ASVAB STUDY GUIDE

Comprehensive Review with Expert Guidance, Full-Length Practice
Test, and 2500 Online Questions & Answers Explained

Vince J. Marshall

ISBN: Print 9798334542754

Table of Contents

Introduction

Welcome to the ASVAB Study Guide 2025-2026. This guide is designed to be your comprehensive resource for preparing for the Armed Services Vocational Aptitude Battery (ASVAB) exam. Whether you're a high school student, a recent graduate, or someone considering a career change into the military, this guide will provide you with the tools, strategies, and confidence you need to succeed.

In this guide, you will find detailed explanations of the ASVAB test structure, the different domains covered, and the scoring system. Additionally, there are numerous practice questions for each section to help you hone your skills and identify areas for improvement. The guide also includes tips and techniques to manage your time effectively, eliminate wrong answers, and stay calm during the test. To keep you motivated, you will read inspiring stories from individuals who have successfully navigated the ASVAB and pursued fulfilling military careers. Furthermore, recommendations for online resources, books, and apps are provided to further aid your preparation.

To make the most of this guide, start by reading through each chapter to understand what is required comprehensively. Use the practice questions and mock tests provided to test your knowledge and improve your test-taking skills. Track your progress by keeping note of your scores and reviewing the explanations for any questions you get wrong to understand your mistakes. Stay inspired by reading the personal stories and motivational tips sprinkled throughout the guide.

Preparing for the ASVAB can be a daunting task, but with the right mindset and resources, you can achieve a score that opens up numerous opportunities in the military. We are here to support you every step of the way. Good luck, and let's begin your journey to unlock your potential!

Why the ASVAB is Important

The ASVAB is more than just an exam; it is a gateway to your future in the United States military. Here's why it holds such significance:

- **Determining Eligibility**: The ASVAB determines your eligibility for enlistment in the U.S. Armed Forces. Your scores help military recruiters understand your strengths and how you can best serve your country. A higher score increases your chances of qualifying for your desired branch and role.

- **Assessing Aptitude**: The ASVAB assesses your aptitude in various areas, including mathematics, verbal skills, science, technical skills, and spatial reasoning. Your performance in these areas guides military career counselors in placing you into roles where you are most likely to excel and find fulfillment.

- **Identifying Strengths and Weaknesses**: The ASVAB helps you identify your strengths and weaknesses, which is valuable information for your military career and your personal and professional development. Understanding your capabilities allows you to focus on areas needing improvement and effectively leverage your strengths.

- **Opening Doors to Opportunities**: A good ASVAB score can open doors to a wide range of opportunities within the military. From technical and mechanical positions to roles in healthcare, communications, and intelligence, your ASVAB score can significantly influence your career paths.

- **Personal Growth**: Preparing for and taking the ASVAB is more than just a test; it's an opportunity for personal growth. The process encourages discipline, critical thinking, and problem-solving skills, all of which are invaluable in the military and beyond. It's not just about the score, but about the skills and traits you develop along the way.

By understanding the importance of the ASVAB, you can approach your preparation with the seriousness and dedication it deserves. This exam is not just a test of knowledge, but a stepping stone to a rewarding career in the military. Your commitment to preparing for the ASVAB is an investment in your future success, and a comprehensive study guide is your tool to fully understand and conquer this important exam.

Updates for 2025-2026

The ASVAB exam undergoes periodic updates to ensure it remains relevant and effective in evaluating the skills and knowledge necessary for today's military roles. For the 2025-2026 cycle, several key updates have been made to the exam format and content. Understanding these changes is crucial for effective preparation:

- **New Question Types**: The ASVAB has introduced new question types to assess critical thinking and problem-solving abilities better. These questions are designed to reflect real-world scenarios that you may encounter in the military.

- **Revised Subject Areas**: Certain subject areas have been revised to include the latest information and practices. For example, the General Science section now covers more contemporary biology, chemistry, and environmental science topics. Similarly, the Electronics Information section has been updated to include recent technological advancements.

- **Refined Scoring Methodology**: The scoring methodology has been refined to represent a candidate's abilities accurately. This includes changes in how composite scores are calculated and reported, giving a clearer picture of your strengths across different domains.

- **Increased Emphasis on Technical Roles**: With the growing importance of technical roles in the military, there is a greater emphasis on sections like Mechanical Comprehension and Auto & Shop Information. These sections now contain more questions related to modern mechanical and technical concepts.

- **Enhanced Online Testing Capabilities**: In response to the increasing need for flexible testing options, the ASVAB now offers more robust online testing capabilities. This includes better accessibility and accommodations for test-takers who may not be able to attend in-person testing centers.

Staying informed about these updates is crucial for effective preparation. This guide is designed to help you navigate these changes, ensuring that your study efforts are aligned with the current version of the ASVAB and maximizing your chances of achieving a high score.

How to Use This Guide

This guide provides a comprehensive roadmap to preparing for the ASVAB. Here's how to make the most out of each section:

- **Start with the Introductory Chapters**: Begin by reading the introductory chapters to gain a solid understanding of the ASVAB exam, its structure, and its significance. Familiarize yourself with the test format and the different domains it covers.

- **Create a Study Schedule**: Develop a study schedule that fits your lifestyle and allows you to cover all the material in this guide. Consistent, regular study sessions are more effective than cramming all at once.

- **Engage with Practice Questions**: Each chapter includes practice questions designed to test your understanding of the material. Take these practice questions seriously and use them as a tool to identify areas where you need more review.

- **Review Explanations**: After answering practice questions, review the explanations provided for each answer. Understanding why an answer is correct or incorrect will deepen your comprehension of the material.

- **Take Full-Length Practice Tests**: At various points in your preparation, take the full-length practice tests in this guide. These tests simulate the actual exam conditions and help you build stamina and confidence.

- **Identify Weak Areas**: Use the results from your practice tests to identify your weak areas. Devote extra study time to these sections to ensure you are well-prepared across all domains.

- **Stay Motivated**: Read the personal stories and motivational tips sprinkled throughout the guide. These real-life experiences can inspire and remind you that achieving a high ASVAB score is attainable with hard work and dedication.

- **Leverage Additional Resources**: Utilize the additional resources recommended in the appendix. These include online tools, apps, and other books that can supplement your study efforts.

By following these guidelines and utilizing this guide effectively, you will be well on your way to mastering the ASVAB and unlocking the potential for a successful military career.

Chapter 1: Understanding the ASVAB Exam

1.1 Overview of the ASVAB

The Armed Services Vocational Aptitude Battery (ASVAB) is a comprehensive multiple-aptitude test designed to assess your skills and potential for success in military training and various occupational fields. This test not only determines your qualification for enlistment in the United States Armed Forces but also helps identify which military jobs (Military Occupational Specialties - MOS) are best suited for your abilities.

The ASVAB evaluates a candidate's abilities across ten distinct areas:

- **General Science (GS)**: Tests knowledge of life, earth, space, and physical sciences.

- **Arithmetic Reasoning (AR)**: Measures ability to solve basic arithmetic word problems.

- **Word Knowledge (WK)**: Assesses understanding of word meanings through synonyms.

- **Paragraph Comprehension (PC)**: Evaluates ability to obtain information from written material.

- **Mathematics Knowledge (MK)**: Measures knowledge of mathematical concepts and applications.

- **Electronics Information (EI)**: Tests knowledge of electrical currents, circuits, devices, and electronic systems.

- **Auto and Shop Information (AS)**: Assesses knowledge of automotive maintenance and repair, and wood and metal shop practices.

- **Mechanical Comprehension (MC)**: Measures understanding of mechanical and physical principles.

- **Assembling Objects (AO)**: Tests spatial relationship skills by requiring you to determine how an object will look when its parts are put together.

- **Verbal Expression (VE)**: A combined score of Word Knowledge and Paragraph Comprehension.

Each of these subtests provides a comprehensive assessment that helps match individuals with appropriate career paths in the military.

1.2 Structure and Format of the Exam

The ASVAB is administered in two formats: computerized (CAT-ASVAB) and paper-and-pencil (P&P-ASVAB). Both formats cover the same content areas but differ in their administration and timing.

CAT-ASVAB: This is an adaptive test, meaning the difficulty of questions adjusts based on your responses. It typically takes about 1.5 hours to complete. The adaptive nature of the test allows for a more accurate assessment of your abilities in a shorter amount of time.

P&P-ASVAB: This traditional format is not adaptive and consists of fixed questions. It takes about 3 hours to complete. While not adaptive, it allows you to skip questions and return to them later, which can be advantageous for those who manage their time well.

Each subtest in both formats measures specific skills and knowledge:

Subtest	Number of Questions (CAT)	Time (CAT)	Number of Questions (P&P)	Time (P&P)
General Science (GS)	16	8 minutes	25	11 minutes
Arithmetic Reasoning (AR)	16	39 minutes	30	36 minutes
Word Knowledge (WK)	16	8 minutes	35	11 minutes
Paragraph Comprehension (PC)	11	22 minutes	15	13 minutes
Mathematics Knowledge (MK)	16	20 minutes	25	24 minutes
Electronics Information (EI)	16	8 minutes	20	9 minutes
Auto and Shop Information (AS)	11	7 minutes	25	11 minutes
Mechanical Comprehension (MC)	16	20 minutes	25	19 minutes
Assembling Objects (AO)	16	16 minutes	25	15 minutes

1.3 Types of ASVAB Tests

There are three primary versions of the ASVAB:

1. **CAT-ASVAB (Computerized Adaptive Test)**: Administered at Military Entrance Processing Stations (MEPS), this version is adaptive and adjusts the difficulty of questions based on your answers. It provides immediate results upon completion. The CAT-ASVAB is designed to be more efficient and typically takes less time to complete than the paper-and-pencil version. This format enhances the accuracy of assessing your abilities, tailoring the test to your performance level.

2. **MET-site ASVAB (Mobile Examination Test)**: This paper-and-pencil version is administered at various mobile testing centers, including high schools and colleges. Unlike the CAT-ASVAB, it does not adapt to your ability level and requires manual scoring, which can take a few days. This version is particularly useful for those who might not have access to a MEPS facility.

3. **P&P-ASVAB (Paper and Pencil)**: Administered at Military Entrance Test (MET) sites and other locations, this traditional format is fixed and does not adapt to the test-taker's ability. It takes about three hours to complete and allows you to skip questions and return to them later, which can be advantageous for those who prefer to manage their time by answering easier questions first and returning to more challenging ones later.

Understanding the format and type of ASVAB you will be taking is essential for effective preparation. Each format requires a slightly different approach to test-taking strategies and time management. For instance, the CAT-ASVAB's adaptive nature means you should focus on each question thoroughly, as you cannot go back to change your answers. In contrast, the P&P-ASVAB allows for review and changes, making time management a critical component of your test-taking strategy.

1.4 Scoring and Interpretation

The ASVAB scoring system is designed to provide a detailed profile of your strengths and areas for improvement. Each subtest produces a Standard Score, indicating how well you performed relative to a national test-taker sample. These Standard Scores are then used to calculate various composite scores.

Armed Forces Qualification Test (AFQT) Score: The most crucial score derived from the ASVAB is the Armed Forces Qualification Test (AFQT) score, which determines your eligibility for enlistment. The AFQT score is calculated using the Standard Scores from four subtests:

- **Arithmetic Reasoning (AR)**
- **Mathematics Knowledge (MK)**
- **Paragraph Comprehension (PC)**
- **Word Knowledge (WK)**

This score is reported as a percentile between 1 and 99, indicating how you performed relative to others. For example, an AFQT score of 65 means you scored better than 65% of the national sample. Each branch of the military has its own minimum AFQT score requirements which must be met for enlistment.

Composite Scores: More than just numbers, the ASVAB composite scores, in addition to the AFQT score, are the gateway to specific military jobs. Each branch of the military has its own set of composite scores and requirements for various Military Occupational Specialties (MOS).
Composite scores are calculated by combining the Standard Scores from specific subtests. For example:

Army Clerical (CL): Composed of Verbal Expression (VE), Arithmetic Reasoning (AR), and Mathematics Knowledge (MK) scores.

- **Navy Mechanical Maintenance (MM)**: Composed of General Science (GS), Arithmetic Reasoning (AR), Mechanical Comprehension (MC), and Electronics Information (EI) scores.

These composite scores help military career counselors determine which jobs you are best suited for based on your unique strengths and abilities.

Understanding your AFQT score and composite scores is crucial for your military career planning. These scores not only determine your eligibility but also influence the range of job opportunities available to you in the Armed Forces. By comprehending the structure, scoring, and significance of the ASVAB and AFQT scores, you can better prepare yourself for the exam and position yourself for success in your military career. This understanding also opens up a world of potential for growth and advancement in the Armed Forces, giving you hope and optimism for your future.

1.5 Understanding Composite Scores

In addition to the Armed Forces Qualification Test (AFQT) score, the ASVAB generates several composite scores, also known as line scores. These scores are crucial as they determine your qualification for specific military jobs. Each military branch has its own composite scores and requirements for various Military Occupational Specialties (MOS).

Composite Scores Calculation: Composite scores are calculated by combining the Standard Scores from specific subtests. Here are examples for different branches of the military:

Branch	Composite Score	Subtests
Army	Clerical (CL)	Verbal Expression (VE) + Arithmetic Reasoning (AR) + Mathematics Knowledge (MK)
	Combat (CO)	Arithmetic Reasoning (AR) + Coding Speed (CS) + Mathematics Knowledge (MK) + Verbal Expression (VE)
	Electronics (EL)	General Science (GS) + Arithmetic Reasoning (AR) + Mathematics Knowledge (MK) + Electronics Information (EI)
	General Technical (GT)	Verbal Expression (VE) + Arithmetic Reasoning (AR)
	Mechanical Maintenance (MM)	Numerical Operations (NO) + Auto & Shop Information (AS) + Mechanical Comprehension (MC) + Electronics Information (EI)
	Skilled Technical (ST)	General Science (GS) + Verbal Expression (VE) + Mathematics Knowledge (MK) + Mechanical Comprehension (MC)
Navy	Engineering and Physical Science (EP)	Arithmetic Reasoning (AR) + Mathematics Knowledge (MK) + Electronics Information (EI) + General Science (GS)
	General Technical (GT)	Verbal Expression (VE) + Arithmetic Reasoning (AR)
	Mechanical Maintenance (MM)	Arithmetic Reasoning (AR) + Verbal Expression (VE) + Auto & Shop Information (AS) + Mechanical Comprehension (MC)
	Nuclear Field (NF)	Arithmetic Reasoning (AR) + Mathematics Knowledge (MK) + Electronics Information (EI) + General Science (GS)
Air Force	Administrative (A)	Verbal Expression (VE) + Mathematics Knowledge (MK)
	Electronics (E)	Arithmetic Reasoning (AR) + Mathematics Knowledge (MK) + Electronics Information (EI) + General Science (GS)
	General (G)	Verbal Expression (VE) + Arithmetic Reasoning (AR)
	Mechanical (M)	Mechanical Comprehension (MC) + Auto & Shop Information (AS) + Arithmetic Reasoning (AR) + Mathematics Knowledge (MK)
Marine Corps	General Technical (GT)	Verbal Expression (VE) + Arithmetic Reasoning (AR)
	Electronics Repair (EL)	General Science (GS) + Arithmetic Reasoning (AR) + Mathematics Knowledge (MK) + Electronics Information (EI)
	Mechanical Maintenance (MM)	Numerical Operations (NO) + Auto & Shop Information (AS) + Mechanical Comprehension (MC) + Electronics Information (EI)
	Clerical (CL)	Verbal Expression (VE) + Arithmetic Reasoning (AR) + Mathematics Knowledge (MK)
	Skilled Technical (ST)	General Science (GS) + Verbal Expression (VE) + Mathematics Knowledge (MK) + Mechanical Comprehension (MC)

1.6 The Role of the AFQT Score

The Armed Forces Qualification Test (AFQT) score plays a pivotal role in enlistment. It is the primary measure to determine your eligibility to join the military. The AFQT score is a composite score derived from four ASVAB subtests:

Subtest
Arithmetic Reasoning (AR)
Mathematics Knowledge (MK)
Paragraph Comprehension (PC)
Word Knowledge (WK)

The AFQT score is a percentile, which compares your performance to a nationally representative sample of 18 to 23-year-olds. A higher AFQT percentile indicates better performance relative to the sample population. Here is how the minimum AFQT score requirements vary by branch:

Military Branch	Minimum AFQT Score
Army	31
Navy	35
Air Force	36
Marine Corps	32
Coast Guard	40

A higher AFQT score can open up more opportunities for advanced training and specialized roles within the military. Your AFQT score also influences the range of job opportunities available to you.

It is important to note that these scores are for applicants with a high school diploma. For those with a GED, the required scores are generally higher. For example, GED holders often need to score at least 50 on the AFQT to be eligible for enlistment in any branch.

These higher score requirements for GED holders are intended to ensure that recruits possess the necessary academic foundation and skills for military service, compensating for the lack of a traditional high school diploma. This also aligns with the military's goal to maintain a high standard of recruits capable of handling military training and service demands.

Chapter 2: Building a Strong Foundation

2.1. Introduction to the Four Domains

The ASVAB test measures a wide range of skills and aptitudes through four main domains: Verbal, Math, Science and Technical, and Spatial. Understanding these domains and their subtests is crucial for effective preparation.

- **Verbal Domain**: This area assesses your ability to understand and interpret written material as well as your vocabulary knowledge. It includes subtests that measure how well you can comprehend paragraphs and identify t

- he meanings of words. Strong verbal skills are essential for effective communication and understanding instructions in both military and everyday contexts.

- **Math Domain**: This category evaluates your numerical reasoning and mathematical problem-solving abilities. It includes subtests focused on arithmetic reasoning and knowledge of mathematical concepts such as algebra and geometry. Proficiency in math is vital for technical tasks and logical problem-solving in many military roles.

- **Science and Technical Domain**: This section measures your understanding of scientific principles and technical information, which are critical for many military occupations. It includes subtests on general science, electronics information, auto and shop information, and mechanical comprehension. These areas are fundamental for roles that involve technical and mechanical skills.

- **Spatial Domain**: This portion tests your ability to visualize and manipulate objects in space. The subtest for this domain is Assembling Objects, which assesses how well you can determine how different parts fit together to form a whole. Spatial reasoning skills are crucial for tasks that involve assembling and repairing equipment.

By mastering these domains, you can ensure a well-rounded performance on the ASVAB, increasing your chances of qualifying for a wide range of military jobs.

2.2 Verbal Domain Overview

The Verbal Domain focuses on your ability to understand and process written information, which is essential for communication and comprehension in any military role. This domain includes two subtests:

- **Word Knowledge (WK)**: This subtest measures your ability to understand the meaning of words through synonyms. A strong vocabulary is crucial as it enables you to comprehend orders, technical manuals, and other important documents. Improving your vocabulary involves reading widely from various sources, keeping a vocabulary journal, and using flashcards to regularly review and reinforce your understanding of new words.

- **Paragraph Comprehension (PC)**: This subtest evaluates your ability to obtain information from written material. It involves reading passages and answering questions about the main ideas, details, and inferences. Effective reading comprehension skills are vital for following written instructions and understanding briefings. To excel in this subtest, practice summarizing paragraphs, identifying main ideas and supporting details, and making inferences based on the text.

Strategies for Success

- **Expand Your Vocabulary**: Read a variety of texts, such as books, articles, and technical manuals, to encounter new words. Maintain a vocabulary journal to track and review these words.

- **Practice Reading Comprehension**: Regularly practice with sample passages and questions. Focus on identifying the main ideas, supporting details, and making logical inferences.

- **Use Context Clues**: When encountering unfamiliar words, use context clues from the surrounding text to infer their meanings.

- **Engage with Diverse Materials**: Read materials related to different subjects to build a versatile vocabulary and improve your ability to understand various types of content.

2.3 Math Domain Overview

The Math Domain assesses your numerical reasoning and mathematical problem-solving abilities. This domain includes two subtests:

Arithmetic Reasoning (AR): This subtest measures your ability to solve arithmetic word problems. These problems often involve real-life scenarios that require you to apply basic mathematical operations and reasoning skills. To excel in Arithmetic Reasoning, practice solving a variety of word problems, focus on understanding the problem's context, and break down the problem into manageable steps. Familiarize yourself with common mathematical operations and practice mental math to increase your speed and accuracy.

Mathematics Knowledge (MK): This subtest evaluates your understanding of mathematical concepts, including algebra and geometry. A solid grasp of these concepts is essential for technical tasks and problem-solving in various military roles. To improve in Mathematics Knowledge, review fundamental algebraic and geometric principles, practice solving equations, and work on problems involving shapes, angles, and formulas. Use online resources and practice tests to reinforce your understanding and identify areas for improvement.

Strategies for Success:

- **Understand Basic Concepts**: Review and master basic arithmetic, algebra, and geometry concepts. Use textbooks, online resources, and practice problems to reinforce your understanding.

- **Practice Word Problems**: Regularly practice solving word problems to improve your ability to apply mathematical concepts to real-life scenarios.

- **Break Down Problems**: Break down complex problems into smaller, more manageable steps to avoid feeling overwhelmed and to ensure accuracy.

- **Use Study Aids**: Utilize study aids such as flashcards, apps, and online tutorials to reinforce key concepts and improve problem-solving skills.

2.4 Science and Technical Domain Overview

The Science and Technical Domain measures your knowledge of scientific principles and technical information, which are critical for many military occupations. This domain includes four subtests:

General Science (GS): This subtest assesses your understanding of basic scientific concepts, including biology, chemistry, physics, and earth science. To excel in General Science, review fundamental principles in each of these areas, use study guides, and take practice tests to gauge your knowledge. Focus on understanding key concepts and their applications in real-world scenarios.

Electronics Information (EI): This subtest measures your knowledge of electrical currents, circuits, devices, and electronic systems. To improve in Electronics Information, study the basics of electronics, including Ohm's Law, circuit components, and common electronic devices. Use practical examples and hands-on projects to reinforce your understanding.

Auto and Shop Information (AS): This subtest evaluates your knowledge of automotive maintenance, repair, and shop practices. Review common automotive systems, tools, and maintenance procedures.

Hands-on experience with automotive repair and shop projects can greatly enhance your understanding and performance in this subtest.

Mechanical Comprehension (MC): This subtest measures your understanding of mechanical principles and devices. Study basic mechanics, including the principles of force, motion, and energy. Practice problems involving levers, pulleys, gears, and other mechanical devices to strengthen your comprehension.

Strategies for Success

- **Review Fundamental Concepts**: Use textbooks, online resources, and study guides to review basic principles in each scientific and technical area.

- **Hands-On Practice**: Engage in hands-on projects and practical applications to reinforce your understanding of mechanical and electronic concepts.

- **Use Visual Aids**: Utilize diagrams, videos, and interactive tools to visualize scientific and technical principles.

- **Practice Regularly**: Regularly practice with sample questions and problems to improve your understanding and test-taking skills.

2.5 Spatial Domain Overview

The Spatial Domain assesses your ability to visualize and manipulate objects in space, which is important for many technical and mechanical roles in the military. This domain includes one subtest:

Assembling Objects (AO): This subtest measures your ability to determine how different parts fit together to form a whole object. Spatial reasoning skills are crucial for tasks that involve assembling and repairing equipment.

Strategies for Success

- **Practice with Puzzles**: Engage in puzzles like jigsaw puzzles, 3D puzzles, and spatial reasoning games to enhance your visualization skills.

- **Visualize and Manipulate Objects**: Work on exercises that involve visualizing and manipulating objects in space, such as model building and origami.

- **Use Study Aids**: Use online resources, apps, and practice tests focusing on spatial reasoning to improve your performance.
- **Hands-On Activities**: Participate in hands-on activities that require spatial awareness, such as assembling furniture or working with tools.

We Value Your Feedback!

We're confident that our ASVAB Study Guide and bonus materials will help you succeed on your exam.

Your success is our priority, and we hope these resources are making your study journey easier and more effective.

If you've found our guide beneficial, we'd love to hear your thoughts! Leaving an honest review on Amazon not only helps us continue to improve our products but also guides other students in choosing the right resources.

Thank you for your support, and we wish you the best of luck with your studies!

TO LEAVE YOUR REVIEW

SCAN THE CODE

SCAN ME

Chapter 3: Mathematics Mastery

3.1 Arithmetic Reasoning

Arithmetic Reasoning (AR) tests your ability to solve basic arithmetic word problems. This subtest evaluates your numerical reasoning skills and your ability to apply mathematical concepts to real-life scenarios. It is crucial for many military tasks that require quick and accurate calculations.

Tips and Techniques

- **Understand the Problem**: Carefully read the problem to understand what is being asked. Identify the key information and what you need to find. Look for keywords that indicate mathematical operations, such as "total," "difference," "product," or "quotient."

- **Break It Down**: Break down the problem into smaller, manageable steps. This can help you avoid mistakes and make the problem easier to solve. For instance, if a problem involves multiple steps, tackle each part one at a time.

- **Use Estimation**: Sometimes, estimating the answer can help you quickly eliminate incorrect options and narrow down the choices. Estimation is particularly useful in multiple-choice questions where you can often eliminate some of the choices that are far off.

- **Check Your Work**: After solving the problem, review your calculations to ensure accuracy. This can help catch any errors before you move on. Double-check your steps and make sure the answer makes sense in the context of the problem.

- **Practice Regularly**: The more you practice, the more familiar you will become with different types of problems, which can help increase your speed and confidence. Use practice tests and sample problems to build your skills.

Core Concepts

- **Basic Operations**:
    - **Addition**: Combining two or more numbers to get a total.
    - **Subtraction**: Finding the difference between two numbers.
    - **Multiplication**: Finding the total when one number is taken a certain number of times.
    - **Division**: Splitting a number into equal parts.

- **Fractions and Decimals**:
  - o **Converting**: Understanding how to convert between fractions, decimals, and percentages.
  - o **Operations**: Performing addition, subtraction, multiplication, and division with fractions and decimals.

- **Ratios and Proportions**:
  - o **Ratios**: A comparison between two quantities.
  - o **Proportions**: An equation stating that two ratios are equal.
  - o **Percentages**:
  - o **Calculations**: Finding percentages, percentage increase/decrease, and solving problems involving discounts and interest.

- **Word Problems**:
  - o **Translation**: Converting verbal descriptions into mathematical expressions and equations.
  - o **Solving**: Applying mathematical operations to solve the problem.

Detailed Sample Questions and Explanations

1. **Problem**: If a car travels at a speed of 60 miles per hour, how long will it take to travel 180 miles?
   - o **Solution**: To find the time, use the formula: $\text{Time} = \frac{\text{Distance}}{\text{Speed}}$

   $$\text{Time} = \frac{180 \text{ miles}}{60 \text{ miles per hour}} = 3 \text{ hours}$$

   - o **Explanation**: The car will take 3 hours to travel 180 miles at a speed of 60 miles per hour. This problem involves basic division.

2. **Problem**: A store sells apples for $0.75 each. If a customer buys 12 apples, how much will it cost?
   - o **Solution**: To find the total cost, multiply the number of apples by the price per apple.

   $$\text{Total Cost} = 12 \text{ apples} \times 0.75 \text{ per apple} = 9.00$$

   - o **Explanation**: The total cost for 12 apples at $0.75 each is $9.00. This problem involves basic   multiplication.

3. **Problem**: If a rectangle has a length of 8 meters and a width of 5 meters, what is its area?
   - o **Solution**: To find the area of a rectangle, use the formula: $\text{Area} = \text{Length} \times \text{Width}$.

   $$\text{Area} = 8 \text{ meters} \times 5 \text{ meters} = 40 \text{ square meters}$$

- o **Explanation**: The area of the rectangle is 40 square meters. This problem involves basic multiplication of dimensions.

4. **Problem**: John has 3/4 of a cake. He eats 1/3 of what he has. How much cake does he have left?
   - o **Solution**: To find out how much cake John has left, multiply the fraction of the cake he has by the fraction he eats: $\left(\frac{3}{4}\right) \times \left(\frac{1}{3}\right) = \frac{3}{12} = \frac{1}{4}$

     Subtract the portion he eats from the total he had: $\frac{3}{4} - \frac{1}{4} = \frac{2}{4} = \frac{1}{2}$
   - o **Explanation**: John has 1/2 of the cake left after eating 1/3 of what he had. This problem involves multiplication and subtraction of fractions.

5. **Problem**: A recipe calls for 2/3 cup of sugar. If you want to make half of the recipe, how much sugar do you need?
   - o **Solution**: To find out how much sugar is needed for half the recipe, multiply the amount of sugar by $\frac{1}{2}$:

     $$\left(\frac{2}{3}\right) \times \left(\frac{1}{2}\right) = \frac{2}{6} = \frac{1}{3}$$
   - o **Explanation**: You need $\frac{1}{3}$ cup of sugar to make half of the recipe. This problem involves multiplication of fractions.

6. **Problem**: A train travels 150 miles in 2.5 hours. What is its average speed?
   - o **Solution**: $Average\ Speed = \frac{\text{Distance}}{\text{Time}}$

     $Average\ Speed = \frac{150 \text{ miles}}{2.5 \text{ hours}} = 60 \text{ miles per hour}$
   - o **Explanation**: The train's average speed is 60 miles per hour. This problem involves division.

7. **Problem**: If a recipe requires 4 cups of flour to make 2 loaves of bread, how many cups of flour are needed to make 5 loaves?
   - o **Solution**: $\frac{4 \text{ cups}}{2 \text{ loaves}} = \frac{x \text{ cups}}{5 \text{ loaves}}$

     Cross-multiply and solve for x: $4 \times 5 = 2 \times x \Rightarrow 20 = 2x \Rightarrow x = 10$
   - o **Explanation**: You need 10 cups of flour to make 5 loaves of bread. This problem involves setting up and solving a proportion.

8. **Problem**: A phone is discounted by 20%, and its sale price is $240. What was the original price?

   o **Solution**: Let the original price be x.

   A 20% discount means the sale price is 80% of the original price.

   $$0.8x = 240 \Rightarrow x = \frac{240}{0.8} = 300$$

   o **Explanation**: The original price of the phone was $300. This problem involves solving a percentage problem.

9. **Problem**: If a worker earns $15 per hour and works 40 hours a week, what is his weekly income?

   o **Solution**: *Weekly Income* = Hourly Rate × Hours Worked

   Weekly Income = 15/hour × 40 hours = 600

   o **Explanation**: The worker's weekly income is $600. This problem involves multiplication.

10. **Problem**: If a tank holds 50 gallons of water and is filled at a rate of 5 gallons per minute, how long will it take to fill the tank?

    o **Solution**: To find the time, use the formula: Time $= \frac{\text{Total Volume}}{\text{Rate}}$

    $$\text{Time} = \frac{50 \text{ gallons}}{5 \text{ gallons per minute}} = 10 \text{ minutes}$$

    o **Explanation**: It will take 10 minutes to fill the tank. This problem involves division.

11. **Problem**: A student scored 75%, 80%, and 85% on three tests. What is the student's average score?

    o **Solution**: To find the average score, use the formula: Average Score $= \frac{\text{Sum of Scores}}{\text{Number of Tests}}$

    $$\text{Average Score} = \frac{75 + 80 + 85}{3} = \frac{240}{3} = 80\%$$

    o **Explanation**: The student's average score is 80%. This problem involves finding the mean.

12. **Problem**: A car uses 12 gallons of gas to travel 300 miles. What is the car's fuel efficiency in miles per gallon?

   o **Solution**: $[\text{Fuel Efficiency} = \frac{\text{Distance}}{\text{Fuel Used}}]$

   $$[\text{Fuel Efficiency} = \frac{300 \text{ miles}}{12 \text{ gallons}} = 25 \text{ miles per gallon}]$$

   o **Explanation**: The car's fuel efficiency is 25 miles per gallon. This problem involves division.

13. **Problem**: A bag contains 3 red balls, 2 blue balls, and 5 green balls. What is the probability of drawing a red ball?

   o **Solution**: $[\text{Probability} = \frac{\text{Number of Desired Outcomes}}{\text{Total Number of Outcomes}}]$

   $$[\text{Probability} = \frac{3}{3+2+5} = \frac{3}{10} = 0.3 \text{ or } 30\backslash\%$$

   o **Explanation**: The probability of drawing a red ball is 30%. This problem involves calculating probability.

3.2 Mathematics Knowledge

Mathematics Knowledge (MK) tests your understanding of mathematical concepts and your ability to apply them. This subtest covers a range of topics, including algebra, geometry, number theory, and basic statistics. Mastery of these topics is essential for technical tasks and logical problem-solving in many military roles.

Core Concepts

1. **Basic Algebra**: Understand how to manipulate algebraic expressions and solve equations.
   - **Linear Equations**: Equations of the first degree, which have variables raised to the power of one. They take the form $ax + b = c$.
   - **Inequalities**: Mathematical statements that relate expressions using inequality symbols like $<, >, \leq, \geq$.
   - **Quadratic Equations**: Equations of the second degree, typically in the form $ax^2 + bx + c = 0$

2. **Geometry**: Familiarize yourself with the properties of shapes, theorems, and formulas for calculating area, volume, and perimeter.
   - **Triangles**: Understanding different types of triangles (equilateral, isosceles, scalene) and their properties.
   - **Circles**: Knowing the formulas for the circumference and area of a circle.
   - **Polygons**: Recognizing various polygons and calculating their perimeters and areas.

3. **Number Theory**: Understand the properties of numbers, including factors, multiples, primes, and integers.
   - **Factors and Multiples**: Identifying the factors of a number and understanding least common multiples.
   - **Prime Numbers**: Numbers greater than 1 that have no positive divisors other than 1 and themselves.
   - **Integers**: Whole numbers and their opposites.

4. **Statistics and Probability**: Learn how to interpret data, calculate mean, median, mode, and understand basic probability concepts.

- o **Mean**: The average of a set of numbers.
- o **Median**: The middle value in a set of numbers.
- o **Mode**: The most frequently occurring number in a set.
- o **Basic Probability**: Understanding probability as a measure of the likelihood of an event occurring.

Detailed Examples and Explanations

1. **Solving Linear Equations**:
   - o **Example**: Solve for x : $2x + 3 = 11$
   - o **Solution**: Subtract 3 from both sides: $2x = 8$. Then, divide by 2: $x = 4$
   - o **Explanation**: Isolate the variable xxx by performing inverse operations. First, eliminate the constant term by subtracting it from both sides. Then, solve for x by dividing both sides by the coefficient of x.

2. **Understanding Quadratic Equations**:
   - o **Example**: Solve for x: $x^2 - 4x - 5 = 0$
   - o **Solution**: Factor the equation: $(x - 5)(x + 1) = 0$.

     Then solve for x :
     $$x - 5 = 0 \quad \Rightarrow \quad x = 5$$
     $$x + 1 = 0 \quad \Rightarrow \quad x = -1$$

   - o **Explanation**: Factor the quadratic equation into two binomials. Set each binomial equal to zero and solve for x.

3. **Calculating the Area of a Circle**:
   - o **Example**: Find the area of a circle with a radius of 3 meters.
   - o **Solution**: Use the formula: $Area\} = \pi r^\wedge 2$

     Substitute the radius into the formula: $Area = \pi \times (3 \text{ meters})^2 = 9\pi$ square meters $\approx$ 28.27 square meters

o   **Explanation**: The formula for the area of a circle is π times the square of the radius. Substitute the radius into the formula and calculate the area.

4.   **Finding the Perimeter of a Triangle**:

o   **Example**: Find the perimeter of a triangle with sides measuring 5 meters, 12 meters, and 13 meters.

o   **Solution**: To find the perimeter, add the lengths of all sides.

$$Perimeter = 5 \text{ meters} + 12 \text{ meters} + 13 \text{ meters} = 30 \text{ meters}$$

o   **Explanation**: The perimeter of a triangle is the sum of the lengths of its sides.

5.   **Calculating the Volume of a Rectangular Prism**:

o   **Example**: A box has a length of 4 feet, a width of 3 feet, and a height of 2 feet. What is its volume?

o   **Solution**: Use the formula for the volume of a rectangular prism:

$$Volume = \text{Length} \times \text{Width} \times \text{Height}$$

Substitute the given values into the formula:

$$Volume = 4 \text{ feet} \times 3 \text{ feet} \times 2 \text{ feet} = 24 \text{ cubic feet}$$

o   **Explanation**: The volume of a rectangular prism is the product of its length, width, and height.

Practice Questions with Explanations:

1.   **Problem**: Solve for y : $3y - 7 = 2$

o   **Solution**: Add 7 to both sides: $3y - 7 + 7 = 2 + 7$

$$3y = 9$$

Then, divide by 3: $y = \frac{9}{3}$

$$y = 3$$

Explanation: The value of y that satisfies the equation is 3. Isolate the variable by performing inverse operations.

2. **Problem**: Find the area of a triangle with a base of 6 meters and a height of 4 meters.

   o **Solution**: Use the formula for the area of a triangle: $Area = \frac{1}{2} \times$ Base $\times$ Height.

   Substitute the given values into the formula:

   $$\text{Area} = \frac{1}{2} \times 6 \text{ meters} \times 4 \text{ meters} = 12 \text{ square meters}$$

   o **Explanation**: The area of a triangle is half the product of its base and height.

3. **Problem**: A cylindrical tank has a radius of 2 meters and a height of 5 meters. What is its volume?

   o **Solution**: Use the formula for the volume of a cylinder: $Volume = \pi r^2 h$.

   Substitute the given values into the formula:

   $$Volume = \pi \times (2 \text{ meters})^2 \times 5 \text{ meters} = 20\pi \text{ cubic meters} \approx 62.83 \text{ cubic meters}$$

   o **Explanation**: The volume of a cylinder is the product of π, the square of the radius, and the height.

4. **Problem**: Solve for x: $(4(x - 3) = 2x + 6$

   o **Solution**: Distribute and simplify: $4x - 12 = 2x + 6$

   Subtract $2x$ from both sides:
   $$4x - 12 - 2x = 2x + 6 - 2x$$

   $$2x - 12 = 6$$

   Add 12 to both sides:

   $$2x - 12 + 12 = 6 + 12$$
   $$2x = 18$$

Divide by 2:

$$x = \frac{18}{2}$$

$$x = 9$$

- ○ **Explanation**: Distribute the 4 on the left side, then move all terms involving x to one side and constants to the other, and solve for x.

5. **Problem**: The average of five numbers is 20. If four of the numbers are 18, 22, 19, and 21, what is the fifth number?

- ○ **Solution**: Let the fifth number be x. The average formula is: $\frac{18+22+19+21+x}{5} = 20$

Multiply both sides by 5 to eliminate the fraction:

$$18 + 22 + 19 + 21 + x = 20 \times 5$$

$$80 + x = 100$$

Subtract 80 from both sides to solve for x:

$$x = 100 - 80$$

$$x = 20$$

- ○ **Explanation**: The fifth number needed to make the average 20 is 20. Multiply the average by the number of values to find the total sum, then subtract the sum of the known values.

By understanding these core concepts and practicing with sample questions, you can improve your mathematical knowledge and reasoning skills, which are crucial for performing well on the ASVAB. Regular practice and a solid grasp of algebra, geometry, number theory, and statistics will enhance your ability to solve a variety of mathematical problems efficiently and accurately.

Chapter 4: Verbal Proficiency

4.1. Word Knowledge

The Word Knowledge (WK) subtest is a crucial assessment of your ability to understand the meaning of words through synonyms. A strong vocabulary is not just a personal asset but a professional necessity for comprehending technical manuals, instructions, and other written material you will encounter in the military. This section will help you expand your vocabulary and improve your ability to decipher word meanings through various strategies and practice questions, thereby preparing you for the linguistic challenges of your military career

Expanding Your Vocabulary

Read Widely: To improve your vocabulary, read from various sources, including books, newspapers, and technical manuals. Exposure to different types of content helps you encounter new words in different contexts.

- **Books**: Choose a blend of fiction and nonfiction. Fiction, in particular, is a treasure trove of creative language use, making it an excellent choice for expanding your vocabulary.
- **Newspapers and Magazines**: These sources provide current language usage and introduce you to new terminology in various fields.
- **Technical Manuals**: Reading manuals and guides can help you understand the vocabulary specific to certain professions and industries.

Keep a Vocabulary Journal: Track new words you encounter and their meanings. Write down the word, its definition, and a sentence using the word. Reviewing this journal regularly can reinforce your understanding and recall.

- **Example Entry**:
  - **Word**: Abate
  - **Definition**: To reduce in amount, degree, or intensity.
  - **Sentence**: The storm finally began to abate, allowing the residents to return to their homes.

Use Flashcards: Create flashcards with the word on one side and its definition and an example sentence on the other. Regularly review these flashcards to reinforce your memory. Digital flashcard apps can be useful for on-the-go practice.

- **Tip**: Use spaced repetition systems (SRS) to ensure you review words at optimal intervals for long-term retention.
- **Engage in Word Games and Apps**: Play word games like Scrabble, crossword puzzles, and word search games. Use vocabulary-building apps that provide daily word challenges and quizzes to keep your learning journey entertaining and engaging.

Commonly Tested Words

The ASVAB frequently tests words that are commonly used in military and technical contexts. Familiarize yourself with these words and their synonyms. Here are some examples:

- **Abate**: To reduce in amount, degree, or intensity.
- **Candid**: Honest and straightforward.
- **Facilitate**: To make easier or less difficult.
- **Plausible**: Seemingly reasonable or probable.
- **Augment**: To increase or make larger.
- **Ostentatious**: Showy or pretentious display.
- **Pragmatic**: Dealing with things sensibly and realistically.
- **Vindicate**: To clear of blame or suspicion.

Context Clues Strategies

When encountering unfamiliar words, use context clues to infer their meanings. Pay attention to the words and sentences surrounding the unfamiliar word. Look for synonyms, antonyms, explanations, and examples to help you understand the word in context.

1. **Synonyms**: Words with similar meanings can provide clues.
   - **Example**: "The *garrulous* man, who was very talkative, dominated the conversation."
     - *Talkative* is a synonym that helps you understand that *garrulous* means excessively talkative.

2. **Antonyms**: Words with opposite meanings can also provide hints.

   o **Example**: "Unlike his outgoing sister, he was very *reticent*."

      ▪ *Outgoing* is an antonym that suggests *reticent* means reserved or quiet.

3. **Definitions or Explanations**: Sometimes the sentence will directly define the word.

   o **Example**: "The *euphoria*, or intense happiness, she felt was evident."

      ▪ The phrase "or intense happiness" defines *euphoria*.

4. **Examples**: Specific examples can clarify the meaning of a word.

   o **Example**: "She had a *voracious* appetite, eating three plates of food."

      ▪ The example of eating three plates of food helps define *voracious* as having a very eager or insatiable appetite.

Sample Questions and Explanations

1. **Problem**: The word "prudent" most nearly means:

   o A. Careful

   o B. Reckless

   o C. Stupid

   o D. Brave

   Solution: A. Careful.

   Explanation: "Prudent" means acting with or showing care and thought for the future.

2. **Problem**: The word "anomaly" most nearly means:

   o A. Normality

   o B. Irregularity

   o C. Predictability

   o D. Usualness

   Solution: B. Irregularity.

   Explanation: "Anomaly" means something that deviates from what is standard, normal, or expected.

3. **Problem**: The word "augment" most nearly means:

   - o   A. Reduce
   - o   B. Strengthen
   - o   C. Increase
   - o   D. Weaken

   Solution: C. Increase.

   Explanation: "Augment" means to increase or make larger.

4. **Problem**: The word "vindicate" most nearly means:

   - o   A. Accuse
   - o   B. Justify
   - o   C. Ignore
   - o   D. Conceal

   Solution: B. Justify.

   Explanation: "Vindicate" means to clear of blame or suspicion.

5. **Problem**: The word "ostentatious" most nearly means:

   - o   A. Humble
   - o   B. Showy
   - o   C. Plain
   - o   D. Reserved

   Solution: B. Showy.

   Explanation: "Ostentatious" means characterized by vulgar or pretentious display; designed to impress or attract notice.

Strategies for Success

- o   **Expand Your Vocabulary**: Continuously add new words to your vocabulary by reading diverse materials. Engage with content that challenges you and introduces new terms.
- o   **Use Context Clues**: Practice using context clues to infer the meaning of unfamiliar words. This skill will help you during the test when you encounter words you do not know.

- o **Practice Regularly**: Use practice tests and flashcards to regularly test your vocabulary knowledge. Review your mistakes to understand where you need improvement.

- o **Engage with Diverse Materials**: Read materials related to different subjects to build a versatile vocabulary and improve your ability to understand various types of content.

- o **Stay Consistent**: Make vocabulary building a regular part of your study routine. Consistency is key to retaining new words and improving your word knowledge over time.

By focusing on these strategies and regularly practicing, you can significantly enhance your verbal skills. These skills are not only essential for performing well on the ASVAB but also for succeeding in your military career.

4.2. Paragraph Comprehension

The Paragraph Comprehension (PC) subtest evaluates your ability to obtain information from written material. This skill is essential for understanding orders, technical manuals, and other documents you will use in the military. Effective reading comprehension involves understanding the main ideas, supporting details, and the ability to make inferences from the text.

Reading for Understanding

1. **Identify the Main Idea**: The main idea is the central point or message the author wants to convey. It is usually found in the first or last sentence of a paragraph but can sometimes be implied rather than stated directly.

   Example: "The rapid advancement of technology has significantly transformed the workplace. Automation and artificial intelligence have streamlined many processes, increasing efficiency and reducing the need for manual labor. However, this shift has also led to concerns about job displacement and the need for new skills in the workforce."

   - o **Main Idea**: The advancement of technology has both positive and negative impacts on the workplace.

2. **Find Supporting Details**: These are pieces of information that explain, prove, or enhance the main idea. They can include facts, examples, statistics, or anecdotes.

   Example: In the passage above, supporting details include:

- o "Automation and artificial intelligence have streamlined many processes, increasing efficiency and reducing the need for manual labor."
- o "This shift has also led to concerns about job displacement and the need for new skills in the workforce."

3. **Make Inferences**: Inferences are logical conclusions based on the information provided in the text. They require you to read between the lines and understand what is implied but not explicitly stated.

   Example: If a passage states, "Many employees are attending training sessions to adapt to new technology," you can infer that the workplace is undergoing technological changes and that employees need new skills.

Strategies for Success

Summarize Paragraphs: After reading a paragraph, summarize it in your own words. This helps ensure that you have grasped the main idea and key details.

- o **Example**: "This paragraph discusses how technology has made workplaces more efficient but also highlights the challenges of job displacement and the need for new skills."

Ask Questions: While reading, ask yourself questions about the content to stay engaged and improve comprehension.

- o **Who** is the paragraph about?
- o **What** is happening?
- o **Why** is this important?
- o **How** does this relate to the main idea?

Look for Signal Words: Signal words help you identify the structure of the text and understand relationships between ideas.

- o **Cause and Effect**: because, therefore, thus, consequently
- o **Contrast**: however, but, on the other hand, although
- o **Addition**: furthermore, moreover, in addition

Practice Active Reading: Engage with the text by highlighting or underlining key points and making notes in the margins. This active engagement helps improve retention and understanding.

Practice Passages and Questions

Passage: "The rapid advancement of technology has significantly transformed the workplace. Automation and artificial intelligence have streamlined many processes, increasing efficiency and reducing the need for manual labor. However, this shift has also led to concerns about job displacement and the need for new skills in the workforce."

Question: What is the main idea of the passage?

> A. Technology has improved efficiency in the workplace.
>
> B. Automation and AI have reduced the need for manual labor.
>
> C. The advancement of technology has both positive and negative impacts on the workplace.
>
> D. New skills are required in the modern workforce.

> **Solution**: C. The advancement of technology has both positive and negative impacts on the workplace.
>
> **Explanation**: The passage discusses both the benefits (increased efficiency) and challenges (job displacement and need for new skills) brought about by technological advancements.

Passage: "The Amazon rainforest is home to an incredibly diverse range of species. This vast ecosystem supports millions of plants, animals, and insects, many of which are not found anywhere else on Earth. However, deforestation poses a significant threat to this biodiversity, as large areas of the forest are cleared for agriculture and development."

Question: Based on the passage, which of the following is a supporting detail?

> A. The Amazon rainforest is home to many unique species.
>
> B. Deforestation threatens the biodiversity of the Amazon.
>
> C. The forest is being cleared for agriculture.
>
> D. All of the above.

> **Solution**: D. All of the above.
>
> **Explanation**: Each option provides a detail that supports the main idea of the passage, which is the importance and threat to the biodiversity of the Amazon rainforest.

Types of Questions

1. **Main Idea Questions**: These questions ask you to identify the primary point or message of the passage.
   o **Example**: What is the main idea of the passage?

2. **Detail Questions**: These questions focus on specific information provided in the passage.
   o **Example**: According to the passage, what is one reason for deforestation in the Amazon rainforest?

3. **Inference Questions**: These questions require you to draw conclusions based on the information given in the passage.
   o **Example**: What can be inferred about the impact of technology on jobs?

4. **Vocabulary in Context Questions**: These questions ask you to determine the meaning of a word based on how it is used in the passage.
   o **Example**: In the passage, what does the word "streamlined" most nearly mean?

Sample Questions and Explanations

- **Problem**: Read the following passage and answer the question.
  o Passage: "The rapid advancement of technology has significantly transformed the workplace. Automation and artificial intelligence have streamlined many processes, increasing efficiency and reducing the need for manual labor. However, this shift has also led to concerns about job displacement and the need for new skills in the workforce."

  Question: What is the main idea of the passage?

   A. Technology has improved efficiency in the workplace.

   B. Automation and AI have reduced the need for manual labor.

   C. The advancement of technology has both positive and negative impacts on the workplace.

   D. New skills are required in the modern workforce.

  Solution: C. The advancement of technology has both positive and negative impacts on the workplace.

  Explanation: The passage discusses both the benefits (increased efficiency), and challenges (job displacement and need for new skills) brought about by technological advancements.

- **Problem**: Based on the passage, which of the following is a supporting detail?

    A. Automation has streamlined many processes.

    B. Job displacement is a major concern.

    C. New skills are needed in the workforce.

    D. All of the above.

    Solution: D. All of the above.

    Explanation: Each option provides a detail that supports the main idea of the passage.

- **Problem**: What can be inferred about the impact of automation on manual labor?

    A. It has no impact on manual labor.

    B. It has increased the need for manual labor.

    C. It has reduced the need for manual labor.

    D. It has made manual labor obsolete.

    Solution: C. It has reduced the need for manual labor.

    Explanation: The passage states that automation and AI have streamlined processes, reducing the need for manual labor.

- **Problem**: In the passage, what does the word "displacement" most nearly mean?

    A. Placement in a new job.

    B. Removal from a current job.

    C. Creation of a new job.

    D. Enhancement of job skills.

    Solution: B. Removal from a current job.

    Explanation: The context of the passage indicates that "displacement" refers to the concern about job loss due to automation.

Practice Regularly: Regular practice with sample passages and questions will improve your reading comprehension skills. Use a variety of practice materials to expose yourself to different types of texts and question formats. Review your answers and explanations to understand your mistakes and learn from them.
Stay Calm and Focused: During the test, stay calm and focused. Read each passage carefully and make sure you understand what is being asked before selecting your answer. Take deep breaths if you start to feel anxious, and remember that you have prepared well.

By following these strategies and practicing regularly, you can enhance your paragraph comprehension skills and perform well on the ASVAB.

4.3. Test-Taking Strategies for Verbal Questions

To excel in the verbal sections of the ASVAB, it's important to employ effective test-taking strategies. Here are some tips to help you perform your best:

Time Management

- o **Allocate Time Wisely**: Divide your time based on the number of questions and sections. Allocate a specific amount of time to each question, and stick to this allocation to ensure you complete all questions.

  Example: If you have 40 questions and 60 minutes, aim to spend about 1.5 minutes per question.

- o **Pace Yourself**: Start with easier questions to build confidence and ensure you have enough time for the more difficult ones. Don't spend too much time on any single question.

  Tip: If you encounter a difficult question, make an educated guess and move on. You can always come back to it if time permits.

- o **Practice with Timers**: Use a timer when practicing to simulate the test environment and improve your pacing skills. This will help you get used to the pressure of timed conditions.

Answer Elimination:

- • **Process of Elimination**: Use the process of elimination to narrow down your answer choices. Eliminate the options that are clearly incorrect, which will increase your chances of selecting the correct answer from the remaining choices. **Example**: If a question asks for a synonym for "benevolent" and the choices are "kind," "cruel," "ignorant," and "lazy," you can eliminate "cruel," "ignorant," and "lazy," leaving "kind" as the correct answer.

- • **Look for Extremes**: Extreme words like "always," "never," "all," or "none" are often incorrect. Be cautious of answer choices that use these terms unless you are certain they are correct.

Context Clues:

- o **Infer Meanings**: When you come across unfamiliar words or phrases, use context clues to infer their meaning. Look at the surrounding words and sentences for hints that can help you understand the meaning.

  Example: "Despite the inclement weather, the picnic continued as planned." The word "inclement" can be inferred to mean unfavorable or bad, as it contrasts with the continuation of the picnic.

- o **Synonyms and Antonyms**: Look for words that have similar or opposite meanings to the unfamiliar word. These can provide clues to the word's meaning.

  Example: "The serene lake was a stark contrast to the bustling city." The word "serene" can be inferred to mean calm or peaceful, as it contrasts with "bustling."

- o **Use Practice Tests**: Regular practice is essential for improving your verbal skills. Use practice tests and sample questions to familiarize yourself with the types of questions you will encounter on the ASVAB.

  Tip: Review your answers and explanations to understand your mistakes and learn from them.

- o **Review Vocabulary**: Continuously expand your vocabulary by reading and using flashcards. Focus on words that are commonly used in military and technical contexts.

- o **Engage with Various Texts**: Read a variety of materials, including fiction, non-fiction, technical manuals, and articles. This will help you become comfortable with different writing styles and vocabularies.

- o **Read Carefully**: During the test, read each question carefully to ensure you understand what is being asked before selecting your answer.

- o **Tip**: Pay attention to keywords and phrases in the questions that indicate what you need to look for in the answer choices.

- o **Manage Test Anxiety**: If you start to feel anxious, take deep breaths and remind yourself that you have prepared well. Staying calm and focused will help you think more clearly and make better decisions. Practice relaxation techniques such as deep breathing or visualization before the test.

- o **Stay Positive**: Maintain a positive attitude throughout the test. Confidence can significantly impact your performance, so believe in your preparation and abilities.

Sample Test-Taking Scenario

- • **Question**: The word "gregarious" most nearly means:

  A. Shy

  B. Friendly

  C. Sad

  D. Angry

- • **Process**:

  Step 1: Eliminate clearly incorrect options. "Sad" and "Angry" don't seem related to the context of "gregarious."

Step 2: Consider the remaining options. "Shy" and "Friendly" are opposites.

Step 3: Use context clues or your own knowledge. "Gregarious" is often used to describe someone who is sociable and enjoys the company of others.

Solution: B. Friendly.

Explanation: "Gregarious" means sociable or enjoying the company of others, so "Friendly" is the best synonym.

- **Question**: The passage states, "The rapid advancement of technology has significantly transformed the workplace. Automation and artificial intelligence have streamlined many processes, increasing efficiency and reducing the need for manual labor." What can be inferred about the impact of technology on jobs?

  A. Technology has made all jobs easier.

  B. Technology has eliminated the need for all jobs.

  C. Technology has increased the need for manual labor.

  D. Technology has reduced the need for some manual labor jobs.

- **Process**:

  Step 1: Eliminate options that don't align with the passage. "All jobs" is too broad.

  Step 2: Focus on the specific impact mentioned. The passage notes a reduction in manual labor.

  Step 3: Choose the option that matches the inference.

Solution: D. Technology has reduced the need for some manual labor jobs.

Explanation: The passage states that automation and AI have reduced the need for manual labor, which implies a reduction in some jobs.

Chapter 5: Science and Technical Knowledge

5.1. General Science

The General Science (GS) subtest measures your knowledge of various scientific disciplines, including biology, chemistry, physics, and earth science. A solid understanding of these basics is crucial for many technical and operational roles in the military.

Basics of Biology, Chemistry, Physics, and Earth Science

Biology

1. **Cell Structure and Function**: Understand the basic components of cells and their functions.
   - **Nucleus**: Acts as the control center of the cell, containing genetic material (DNA) that regulates cellular activities.
   - **Cytoplasm**: The gel-like substance inside the cell that contains organelles and is the site of many metabolic processes.
   - **Cell Membrane**: A selectively permeable barrier that controls the movement of substances in and out of the cell.

2. **Genetics**: Learn about DNA, genes, and heredity, including how traits are passed from one generation to the next.
   - **DNA (Deoxyribonucleic Acid)**: The molecule that carries genetic information.
   - **Genes**: Segments of DNA that determine specific traits.
   - **Heredity**: The transmission of genetic characteristics from parents to offspring.
   - **Mendelian Genetics**: The principles of inheritance first described by Gregor Mendel, including dominant and recessive traits.

3. **Human Body Systems**: Familiarize yourself with major body systems and their functions.
   - **Circulatory System**: Transports blood, nutrients, gases, and wastes.
     - Key components: Heart, blood vessels (arteries, veins, capillaries), blood.
   - **Respiratory System**: Facilitates gas exchange (oxygen and carbon dioxide).
     - Key components: Lungs, trachea, bronchi, diaphragm.

- o **Digestive System**: Breaks down food into nutrients and absorbs them into the bloodstream.
  - Key components: Mouth, esophagus, stomach, intestines, liver, pancreas.
- o **Nervous System**: Controls and coordinates body activities by transmitting signals.
  - Key components: Brain, spinal cord, nerves.

4. **Ecology**: Study ecosystems, food chains, and the impact of human activities on the environment.
   - o **Ecosystems**: Communities of organisms interacting with their physical environment.
   - o **Food Chains and Webs**: The flow of energy and nutrients through an ecosystem.
   - o **Human Impact**: Pollution, deforestation, climate change, and conservation efforts.

Chemistry

1. **Atomic Structure**: Know the parts of an atom and how they determine chemical properties.
   - o **Protons**: Positively charged particles in the nucleus.
   - o **Neutrons**: Neutral particles in the nucleus.
   - o **Electrons**: Negatively charged particles orbiting the nucleus.
   - o **Isotopes**: Variants of elements with different numbers of neutrons.

2. **Periodic Table**: Understand the organization of the periodic table, including groups, periods, and element classifications.
   - o **Groups**: Vertical columns that indicate elements with similar chemical properties.
   - o **Periods**: Horizontal rows that indicate increasing atomic numbers.
   - o **Element Classifications**: Metals (good conductors of heat and electricity), nonmetals (poor conductors), metalloids (properties of both metals and nonmetals).

3. **Chemical Reactions**: Learn about different types of chemical reactions and how to balance chemical equations.
   - o **Synthesis Reactions**: Two or more substances combine to form a new compound.
     - Example: $2H_2 + O_2 \rightarrow 2H_2O$
   - o **Decomposition Reactions**: A single compound breaks down into two or more simpler substances.
     - Example: $2H_2O_2 \rightarrow 2H_2O + O_2$
   - o **Combustion Reactions**: A substance reacts with oxygen, releasing energy in the form of heat and light.

- Example: $CH_4 + 2O_2 \rightarrow CO_2 + 2H_2O$

4. **States of Matter**: Recognize the properties and behavior of solids, liquids, gases, and plasmas.

   o **Solids**: Have a definite shape and volume.

   o **Liquids**: Have a definite volume but take the shape of their container.

   o **Gases**: Have neither a definite shape nor volume, expanding to fill their container.

   o **Plasmas**: Ionized gases that conduct electricity and are affected by magnetic fields.

Physics

1. **Forces and Motion**: Study Newton's laws of motion, the concepts of force, mass, and acceleration, and the principles of work, energy, and power.

   o **Newton's First Law (Inertia)**: An object at rest stays at rest, and an object in motion stays in motion unless acted upon by an external force.

   o **Newton's Second Law**: Force equals mass times acceleration $F = ma$.

   o **Newton's Third Law**: For every action, there is an equal and opposite reaction.

   o **Work**: The product of force and distance $W = Fd$.

   o **Energy**: The capacity to do work (kinetic energy, potential energy).

   o **Power**: The rate at which work is done $P = \frac{W}{t}$.

2. **Waves and Light**: Understand the properties of waves and how they apply to sound and light.

   o **Wave Properties**: Frequency, wavelength, amplitude.

   o **Sound Waves**: Longitudinal waves that require a medium to travel.

   o **Light Waves**: Electromagnetic waves that can travel through a vacuum.

   o **Reflection**: Bouncing of light off a surface.

   o **Refraction**: Bending of light as it passes through different mediums.

3. **Electricity and Magnetism**: Learn about electric circuits, voltage, current, resistance, and the relationship between electricity and magnetism.

   o **Ohm's Law**: $V = IR$ (Voltage equals current times resistance).

   o **Series and Parallel Circuits**: Different ways to arrange electrical components.

   o **Magnetic Fields**: Produced by moving electric charges.

   o **Electromagnetism**: Interaction between electric currents and magnetic fields.

Earth Science

1. **Geology**: Familiarize yourself with the structure of the Earth, including the crust, mantle, and core, as well as plate tectonics and the rock cycle.

   o **Crust**: Earth's outer layer.
   o **Mantle**: The thick layer beneath the crust.
   o **Core**: The innermost part of Earth, composed of the outer (liquid) core and inner (solid) core.
   o **Plate Tectonics**: The movement of Earth's lithospheric plates.
   o **Rock Cycle**: The process of rock formation, alteration, and destruction.

2. **Meteorology**: Study weather patterns, atmospheric layers, and the factors that influence climate.

   o **Weather**: The day-to-day state of the atmosphere.
   o **Climate**: The long-term average of weather patterns.
   o **Atmospheric Layers**: Troposphere, stratosphere, mesosphere, thermosphere, exosphere.

3. **Astronomy**: Learn about the solar system, stars, galaxies, and the universe's structure.

   o **Solar System**: Includes the Sun, planets, moons, and other celestial bodies.
   o **Stars**: Luminous spheres of plasma held together by gravity.
   o **Galaxies**: Massive systems of stars, interstellar gas, and dust.
   o **Universe**: The totality of space and all matter and energy within it.

4. **Environmental Science**: Understand human impact on the environment, including pollution, conservation, and sustainable practices.

   o **Pollution**: Contamination of the natural environment.
   o **Conservation**: Efforts to preserve natural resources.
   o **Sustainability**: Practices that ensure resource availability for future generations.

Sample Questions and Explanations

Biology Question: What is the primary function of the mitochondria in a cell?

A. Protein synthesis

B. Photosynthesis

C. Energy production

D. DNA replication

Answer: C. Energy production.

Explanation: The mitochondria are known as the powerhouses of the cell because they produce energy through cellular respiration.

Chemistry Question: Which element is found in group 1 of the periodic table?

A. Helium

B. Sodium

C. Chlorine

D. Iron

Answer: B. Sodium.

Explanation: Sodium (Na) is an alkali metal found in group 1 of the periodic table.

Physics Question: According to Newton's first law of motion, an object in motion will:

A. Accelerate indefinitely.

B. Remain in motion unless acted upon by an external force.

C. Eventually stop due to friction.

D. Change direction when another force is applied.

Answer: B. Remain in motion unless acted upon by an external force.

Explanation: Newton's first law, also known as the law of inertia, states that an object will stay at rest or in uniform motion unless acted upon by an external force.

Earth Science Question: Which layer of the Earth is composed primarily of liquid iron and nickel?

A. Crust

B. Mantle

C. Outer core

D. Inner core

Answer: C. Outer core.

Explanation: The outer core is composed of liquid iron and nickel, which generates Earth's magnetic field.

By mastering the basics of general science, you will be well-prepared for the ASVAB and equipped with the knowledge necessary for various technical roles in the military. Consistent practice and understanding of these concepts are key to achieving a high score in the Science and Technical Knowledge section.

5.2. Electronics Information

The Electronics Information (EI) subtest measures your knowledge of electrical concepts, principles, and terminology. This section is essential for technical roles that involve working with electronic equipment and systems. A strong foundation in electronics will help you excel in various military and technical positions.

Basic Concepts and Principles

1. **Electricity**: Understand the basics of electricity, including voltage (V), current (I), and resistance (R).

   o **Voltage (V)**: The potential difference that drives electric current through a circuit, measured in volts (V).

   o **Current (I)**: The flow of electric charge, measured in amperes (A).

   o **Resistance (R)**: The opposition to the flow of current, measured in ohms (Ω).

2. **Ohm's Law**: The relationship between voltage, current, and resistance in an electrical circuit is given by Ohm's Law: $V = IR$. This fundamental equation helps you calculate one quantity if you know the other two.

   o **Formula**: $V = IR$

   o **Example**: If the voltage across a resistor is 12V and the resistance is 4Ω, the current is

   $$I = \frac{V}{R} = \frac{12V}{4\Omega} = 3A$$

3. **Circuits**: Learn about different types of electrical circuits, including series and parallel circuits, and how to calculate total resistance, current, and voltage in each type.

   o **Series Circuits**: Components are connected end-to-end, so the same current flows through each component. The total resistance is the sum of individual resistances: $R_1 + R_2 + R_3 + \cdots$

   o **Parallel Circuits**: Components are connected across the same voltage source, so the voltage across each component is the same. The total resistance is given by the reciprocal of the sum of reciprocals: $\frac{1}{R_{total}} = \frac{1}{R_1} + \frac{1}{R_2} + \frac{1}{R_3} + \cdots$

47

4. **Components**: Familiarize yourself with common electronic components such as resistors, capacitors, diodes, transistors, and inductors, and their functions within circuits.

   o **Resistors**: Components that oppose the flow of current, used to control voltage and current in a circuit.

   o **Capacitors**: Devices that store electrical energy in an electric field, used to smooth voltage fluctuations and store energy temporarily.

   o **Diodes**: Semiconductors that allow current to flow in one direction only, used for rectification and protection.

   o **Transistors**: Semiconductors used to amplify or switch electronic signals, crucial in digital and analog circuits.

   o **Inductors**: Coils of wire that generate a magnetic field when current flows through them, used in filters and energy storage.

5. **Power**: Understand the concept of electrical power (P) and its calculation using the formula: $P = VI$, where P is power in watts, V is voltage in volts, and I is current in amperes.

   o **Formula**: $P = VI$

   o **Example**: If a device operates at 120V and draws 2A of current, its power consumption is $P = 120V \times 2A = 240W$

6. **AC and DC**: Know the differences between alternating current (AC) and direct current (DC), and the applications of each type in electronic devices and systems.

   o **Direct Current (DC)**: Current flows in one direction, used in batteries and electronic devices.

   o **Alternating Current (AC)**: Current changes direction periodically, used in household and industrial power systems.

   o **Applications**: DC is commonly used in low-voltage applications like electronics, while AC is used for power distribution due to its efficiency over long distances.

Key Terminology

Resistor: A component that opposes the flow of electric current, measured in ohms (Ω).

   o **Function**: Controls the current flow and divides voltage in a circuit.

   o **Symbol**: A zigzag line.

Capacitor: A device that stores electrical energy in an electric field, measured in farads (F).

- o **Function**: Stores and releases energy, smooths out voltage fluctuations.
- o **Symbol**: Two parallel lines with a gap between them.

Inductor: A coil of wire that generates a magnetic field when current flows through it, measured in henries (H).

- o **Function**: Stores energy in a magnetic field, filters signals.
- o **Symbol**: A series of loops or a coiled line.

Diode: A semiconductor device that allows current to flow in one direction only.

- o **Function**: Rectifies AC to DC, protects circuits from reverse voltage.
- o **Symbol**: A triangle pointing to a line.

Transistor: A semiconductor device used to amplify or switch electronic signals.

- o **Function**: Amplifies signals, switches electronic circuits.
- o **Symbol**: Various symbols depending on type (e.g., NPN, PNP).

Practice Questions

1. **Question**: What is the function of a resistor in an electrical circuit?

   A. To store electrical energy

   B. To oppose the flow of current

   C. To amplify signals

   D. To allow current to flow in one direction

   Answer: B. To oppose the flow of current.

   Explanation: A resistor limits the amount of current that can flow through a circuit, thereby protecting other components from excessive current.

2. **Question**: In a series circuit with a total resistance of 10 ohms and a current of 2 amperes, what is the voltage across the circuit?

   A. 5 volts

   B. 10 volts

   C. 20 volts

   D. 40 volts

   Answer: C. 20 volts.

   Explanation: Using Ohm's Law $V = IR$), the voltage is calculated as follows:

   $$V = 2A \times 10\Omega = 20V$$

3. **Question**: What type of current is used in household electrical systems?

    A. Direct current (DC)

    B. Alternating current (AC)

    C. Pulsating DC

    D. Static electricity

    Answer: B. Alternating current (AC).

    Explanation: Household electrical systems use alternating current (AC) because it is more efficient for transmitting electricity over long distances.

4. **Question**: How does a capacitor store electrical energy?

    A. By creating a magnetic field

    B. By storing charge in an electric field

    C. By converting current to voltage

    D. By opposing the flow of current

    Answer: B. By storing charge in an electric field.

    Explanation: A capacitor stores electrical energy by holding a charge on two conductive plates separated by an insulating material.

Question: In a parallel circuit with two resistors of 6 ohms each, what is the total resistance?

    A. 3 ohms

    B. 6 ohms

    C. 12 ohms

    D. 36 ohms

    Answer: A. 3 ohms.

    Explanation: The total resistance of R_{total} of resistors in parallel is found using the formula:

$$\frac{1}{R_{total}} = \frac{1}{R_1} + \frac{1}{R_2}$$

Given:

- $R_1 = 6$
- $R_2 = 6$

Substitute the values into the formula:

$$\frac{1}{R_{total}} = \frac{1}{6} + \frac{1}{6} = \frac{2}{6} = \frac{1}{3}$$

Thus, the total resistance R_{total} is: $R_{total} = \frac{1}{\left(\frac{1}{3}\right)} = 3$ ohms

Advanced Topics and Applications

1. **Transistor Configurations**: Learn about different transistor configurations such as common emitter, common base, and common collector, and their uses in amplification and switching.

   o **Common Emitter**: Used for amplification with high gain.

   o **Common Base**: Provides low input impedance, used in high-frequency applications.

   o **Common Collector**: Used as a buffer with high input impedance and low output impedance.

2. **Digital Electronics**: Understand the basics of digital circuits, including logic gates (AND, OR, NOT), flip-flops, and microcontrollers.

   o **Logic Gates**: Perform basic logical operations essential in digital circuits.

   o **Flip-Flops**: Used for storing binary data.

   o **Microcontrollers**: Integrated circuits used for controlling devices and processes.

3. **Electromagnetic Waves**: Study the generation and propagation of electromagnetic waves, including radio waves, microwaves, infrared, visible light, ultraviolet, X-rays, and gamma rays.

   o **Applications**: Communication (radio, TV), medical imaging (X-rays), and industrial processes.

4. **Signal Processing**: Learn about analog and digital signal processing, including filtering, modulation, and demodulation.

   o **Analog Signals**: Continuous signals that vary over time.

   o **Digital Signals**: Discrete signals used in digital electronics.

   o **Modulation**: Process of varying a carrier signal to transmit data.

   o **Demodulation**: Extracting the original information from a modulated carrier signal.

By mastering these electronics concepts and principles, you will be well-prepared for the ASVAB and equipped with the knowledge necessary for various technical roles in the military. Consistent practice and understanding of these concepts are key to achieving a high score in the Electronics Information section.

5.3. Mechanical Comprehension

The Mechanical Comprehension (MC) subtest measures your understanding of mechanical and physical principles. This section is crucial for roles involving the operation and maintenance of machinery and equipment.

Understanding Mechanical Principles

1. **Levers:** Understand the different types of levers (first-class, second-class, third-class) and how they provide mechanical advantage by changing the direction or magnitude of a force.

2. **Pulleys:** Learn about fixed and movable pulleys, and how pulley systems can be used to lift heavy loads with less effort.

3. **Inclined Planes:** Know how inclined planes reduce the amount of force needed to lift objects by increasing the distance over which the force is applied.

4. **Gears:** Study how gears work, including gear ratios and how they transmit torque and rotational speed between shafts.

5. **Hydraulics and Pneumatics:** Understand the principles of fluid mechanics, including Pascal's law, and how hydraulic and pneumatic systems use fluids to transmit force.

Sample Problems and Explanations:

1. **Question:** Which type of lever has the fulcrum located between the effort and the load?

    A. First-class lever

    B. Second-class lever

    C. Third-class lever

    D. Fourth-class lever

    Answer: A. First-class lever.

    Explanation: In a first-class lever, the fulcrum is positioned between the effort and the load, like a seesaw.

2. **Question:** In a pulley system with two fixed pulleys and one movable pulley, what is the mechanical advantage?

      A. 1

      B. 2

      C. 3

      D. 4

Answer: C. 3.

Explanation: The mechanical advantage of a pulley system is the number of sections of rope supporting the load. In this case, there are three sections, providing a mechanical advantage of 3.

3. **Question:** How does an inclined plane reduce the amount of force needed to lift an object?

      A. By increasing the object's weight

      B. By decreasing the object's weight

      C. By increasing the distance over which the force is applied

      D. By changing the direction of the force

Answer: C. By increasing the distance over which the force is applied.

Explanation: An inclined plane allows you to apply a smaller force over a longer distance to lift an object, reducing the effort needed compared to lifting it vertically.

4. **Question:** If a small gear with 10 teeth drives a larger gear with 50 teeth, what is the gear ratio?

      A. 1:5

      B. 2:5

      C. 5:1

      D. 10:1

Answer: A. 1:5.

Explanation: The gear ratio is determined by dividing the number of teeth on the driven gear by the number of teeth on the driving gear. In this case, $50/10 = 5$, so the ratio is 1:5.

5.4. Auto and Shop Information

The Auto and Shop Information (AS) subtest measures your knowledge of automotive maintenance, repair, and shop practices. This section is essential for roles that involve working with vehicles and machinery. A strong understanding of these concepts will help you excel in various technical positions in the military and civilian sectors.

Basic Auto Maintenance and Repair

- **Engine Components**: Understand the major components of an engine and how they work together to power a vehicle.
  - **Pistons**: Move up and down within the cylinder, driven by the combustion of fuel.
  - **Crankshaft**: Converts the up-and-down motion of the pistons into rotational motion to drive the vehicle's wheels.
  - **Camshaft**: Opens and closes the engine's intake and exhaust valves in sync with the pistons' movements.
  - **Valves**: Allow air and fuel to enter the combustion chamber and exhaust gases to exit.
  - **Spark Plugs**: Ignite the fuel-air mixture in the combustion chamber to create an explosion that drives the pistons.

- **Fuel Systems**: Learn about the components of a fuel system and how they deliver fuel to the engine.
  - **Fuel Pump**: Transfers fuel from the tank to the engine.
  - **Fuel Injectors**: Spray fuel into the engine's combustion chambers at the correct time and amount.
  - **Carburetor**: (in older vehicles) Mixes fuel with air before entering the engine.
  - **Fuel Filter**: Removes contaminants from the fuel before it reaches the engine.

- **Electrical Systems**: Know the basics of a vehicle's electrical system and its key components.
  - **Battery**: Provides electrical power to start the engine and run electrical accessories.
  - **Alternator**: Generates electricity to recharge the battery and power the vehicle's electrical systems while the engine is running.
  - **Starter Motor**: Turns the engine over during starting.
  - **Ignition System**: Includes the spark plugs, ignition coil, distributor, and associated wiring to ignite the fuel-air mixture.
- **Brakes**: Familiarize yourself with different types of brakes and their components.

- o **Disc Brakes**: Use calipers to squeeze brake pads against a rotor to slow down or stop the vehicle.
- o **Drum Brakes**: Use brake shoes to press against the inside of a drum attached to the wheel.
- o **Brake Pads/Shoes**: Provide friction to stop the vehicle.
- o **Rotors/Drums**: The surfaces that the brake pads/shoes press against to slow down or stop the vehicle.
- o **Brake Fluid**: Transfers force from the brake pedal to the brake components.

- **Routine Maintenance**: Understand common maintenance tasks and their importance in keeping a vehicle running smoothly.
  - o **Oil Changes**: Replace the engine oil and oil filter to ensure proper lubrication and prevent engine wear.
  - o **Tire Rotation**: Move tires to different positions on the vehicle to ensure even wear.
  - o **Brake Inspections**: Check the condition of brake pads, rotors, and fluid levels to ensure safe operation.
  - o **Fluid Checks**: Regularly check and top off fluids like coolant, transmission fluid, and power steering fluid.

Tools and Their Uses

- **Hand Tools**: Learn about common hand tools used in automotive and shop environments.
  - o **Wrenches**: Used to turn nuts and bolts. Types include open-end, box-end, and combination wrenches.
  - o **Screwdrivers**: Used to drive screws. Types include flathead, Phillips, and Torx.
  - o **Pliers**: Used for gripping, bending, and cutting wires and other materials. Types include slip-joint, needle-nose, and diagonal pliers.
  - o **Hammers**: Used for driving nails and other fasteners, as well as shaping metal. Types include claw, ball-peen, and mallet.
  - o **Sockets and Ratchets**: Used to turn nuts and bolts with interchangeable sockets for different sizes.

- **Power Tools**: Familiarize yourself with power tools and their applications and safety precautions.
  - o **Drills**: Used for drilling holes in various materials.
  - o **Grinders**: Used for grinding, cutting, and polishing materials.
  - o **Impact Wrenches**: Provide high torque for loosening or tightening nuts and bolts.
  - o **Jigsaws**: Used for making precise cuts in wood, metal, and other materials.

- **Measuring Tools**: Understand the use of measuring tools for precise measurements and adjustments.
  - o **Tape Measures**: Used to measure lengths and distances.
  - o **Calipers**: Provide precise measurements of internal and external dimensions.
  - o **Micrometers**: Used for very precise measurements of small dimensions.
  - o **Torque Wrenches**: Measure and apply specific torque to fasteners.

- **Specialty Tools**: Learn about specialty tools used for specific tasks.
  - o **Spark Plug Wrenches**: Designed for removing and installing spark plugs.
  - o **Oil Filter Wrenches**: Used to remove and install oil filters.
  - o **Brake Bleeders**: Used to remove air from brake lines.

Practice Questions

- **Question**: Which part of the engine converts the up-and-down motion of the pistons into rotational motion?

  A. Crankshaft

  B. Camshaft

  C. Valves

  D. Flywheel

  Answer: A. Crankshaft.

  Explanation: The crankshaft converts the linear motion of the pistons into rotational motion, which drives the vehicle's wheels.

- **Question**: What is the primary function of the alternator in a vehicle's electrical system?

  A. To start the engine

  B. To charge the battery

  C. To ignite the fuel-air mixture

  D. To power the headlights

  Answer: B. To charge the battery.

  Explanation: The alternator generates electricity to charge the battery and power the electrical systems while the engine is running.

- **Question**: Which tool would you use to measure the gap of a spark plug?

  A. Torque wrench

  B. Feeler gauge

  C. Caliper

  D. Micrometer

  Answer: B. Feeler gauge.

  Explanation: A feeler gauge is used to measure the gap between the electrodes of a spark plug to ensure proper ignition.

- **Question**: What type of brake system component applies hydraulic pressure to the brake pads to slow down a vehicle?

  A. Rotor

  B. Caliper

  C. Drum

  D. Axle

Answer: B. Caliper.

Explanation: The caliper applies hydraulic pressure to the brake pads, pressing them against the rotor to slow down or stop the vehicle.

Advanced Topics and Applications

- **Engine Diagnostics**: Learn about the tools and techniques used to diagnose engine problems.
  - **OBD-II Scanner**: A diagnostic tool that reads trouble codes from a vehicle's onboard computer to help identify issues.
  - **Compression Tester**: Measures the compression pressure in an engine's cylinders to check for leaks or other issues.
  - **Vacuum Gauge**: Tests the vacuum pressure in the engine to diagnose problems like leaks or timing issues.

- **Transmission Systems**: Understand the function and components of manual and automatic transmissions.
  - **Manual Transmission**: Uses a clutch and gear shifter to manually change gears.
  - **Automatic Transmission**: Automatically changes gears based on the vehicle's speed and load.
  - **Torque Converter**: A component in automatic transmissions that transfers power from the engine to the transmission.

- **Suspension and Steering**: Study the components and function of a vehicle's suspension and steering systems.
  - o **Shock Absorbers**: Dampen the impact of road irregularities to provide a smooth ride.
  - o **Struts**: Combine a shock absorber and a coil spring to support the vehicle's weight and absorb shocks.
  - o **Steering Rack and Pinion**: Translates the rotation of the steering wheel into the linear motion needed to turn the wheels.

- **Cooling Systems**: Learn about the components and function of a vehicle's cooling system.
  - o **Radiator**: Transfers heat from the engine coolant to the air to prevent overheating.
  - o **Thermostat**: Regulates the flow of coolant to maintain the engine's operating temperature.
  - o **Water Pump**: Circulates coolant through the engine and radiator.

- **Advanced Shop Practices**: Understand advanced techniques and safety practices in a shop environment.
  - o **Welding**: Learn about different types of welding (MIG, TIG, arc) and their applications.
  - o **Metal Fabrication**: Techniques for cutting, bending, and assembling metal components.
  - o **Safety Practices**: Proper use of personal protective equipment (PPE), safe handling of hazardous materials, and maintaining a clean and organized work area.

By mastering these auto and shop concepts and principles, you will be well-prepared for the ASVAB and equipped with the knowledge necessary for various technical roles in the military and civilian sectors. Consistent practice and understanding of these concepts are key to achieving a high score in the Auto and Shop Information section.

Chapter 6: Enhancing Spatial Awareness

6.1. Assembling Objects

The Assembling Objects (AO) subtest evaluates your ability to understand how different parts fit together to form a complete object. This skill is vital for many technical and mechanical roles in the military, where visualizing spatial relationships and components is essential.

Spatial relationships involve recognizing how objects fit together and understanding their positions in space relative to each other. This includes identifying the correct orientation, alignment, and configuration of parts. Improving your ability to comprehend these relationships will enhance your performance on the AO subtest and in practical military tasks.

Visualization Techniques

Mental Rotation: Practice mentally rotating objects to understand how different angles and perspectives affect their appearance. Visualizing objects in various orientations helps you see how parts fit together from different viewpoints.

- o **Exercise**: Use 3D models or drawings and practice imagining them rotating in your mind. Start with simple shapes and gradually increase the complexity.

Diagram Interpretation: Study and interpret diagrams that show how components are assembled. Diagrams often provide a clear visual representation of the steps involved in assembling objects.

- o **Exercise**: Work with assembly manuals for models or furniture, focusing on understanding each step before moving on to the next.

Disassembly and Reassembly: Take apart and reassemble simple objects, such as toys or household items. This hands-on practice can help you understand the spatial relationships between parts and improve your visualization skills.

- o **Exercise**: Disassemble and reassemble common household items like a flashlight or a toy car to see how parts interact.

6.2. Tips for Improving Spatial Reasoning

Improving your spatial reasoning skills requires consistent practice and the use of effective strategies. Here are some tips to help you enhance your spatial reasoning abilities.

1. Practice Regularly

Engaging in regular practice is essential for developing strong spatial reasoning skills. Incorporate a variety of activities into your routine to challenge and improve your abilities.

- **Puzzles and Games**: Engage in activities that challenge your spatial reasoning, such as jigsaw puzzles, 3D puzzles, and video games that involve spatial navigation and problem-solving. These activities help you visualize how pieces fit together and enhance your spatial awareness.

- **Drawing and Sketching**: Practice drawing objects from different perspectives. Sketching helps you visualize spatial relationships and improves your ability to interpret diagrams. Start with simple shapes and gradually move to more complex objects.

- **Spatial Exercises**: Use spatial exercises and brain games designed to enhance your spatial reasoning skills. These exercises often involve mental rotation, pattern recognition, and spatial visualization. Online platforms and apps offer a variety of spatial reasoning exercises to practice.

2. Use Real-World Objects

Working with real-world objects can provide hands-on experience and improve your spatial reasoning abilities.

- **Model Building**: Construct models using building kits, such as LEGO or model airplanes. This hands-on activity helps you understand how parts fit together and improves your spatial visualization skills. Follow detailed instructions to assemble the models, then try creating your own designs.

- **Origami**: Practice origami, the art of paper folding. Origami requires you to visualize and manipulate shapes, enhancing your spatial reasoning abilities. Start with simple folds and progress to more intricate designs.

- **Everyday Tasks**: Perform tasks that involve spatial reasoning, such as rearranging furniture, organizing spaces, or assembling furniture from flat-pack kits. These activities help you practice visualizing how objects fit together and move in space.

3. Develop Visualization Techniques

Effective visualization techniques can significantly improve your spatial reasoning skills.

- **Step-by-Step Visualization**: Break down complex objects into smaller components and visualize each step of the assembly process. This technique helps you manage and understand the spatial relationships between parts. Practice visualizing the assembly steps in your mind before actually putting the parts together.

- **Use Reference Points**: Identify reference points and landmarks in diagrams or real-world objects to help you visualize how parts fit together. Reference points provide a frame of reference that aids in spatial orientation. Use these points to align and orient parts correctly.

- **Practice Mental Rotation**: Regularly practice rotating objects mentally to see how different perspectives affect their appearance. This exercise enhances your ability to visualize objects in three dimensions. Start with simple shapes and gradually move to more complex objects.

4. Apply Spatial Reasoning in Context

Applying spatial reasoning skills in real-world contexts can provide motivation and practical experience.

- **Military Applications**: Consider how spatial reasoning is used in military contexts, such as navigation, map reading, and equipment assembly. Understanding the practical applications of spatial reasoning can motivate you to improve your skills. Study military manuals and practice assembling equipment or navigating using maps.

- **Technical Fields**: Explore how spatial reasoning is applied in technical fields, such as engineering, architecture, and mechanics. Learning about these applications can provide additional context and relevance to your practice. Research projects and case studies that involve spatial reasoning in these fields.

Improving your spatial awareness will not only help you succeed on the ASVAB but also prepare you for various technical and mechanical roles in the military. Consistent practice and a focused approach to understanding spatial relationships are key to mastering this skill.

Chapter 7: Test-Taking Strategies and Tips

7.1. General Test-Taking Strategies

Success on the ASVAB requires more than just knowing the content; it also involves employing effective test-taking strategies. Here are some general strategies to help you maximize your performance:

- **Read Instructions Carefully**: Always read the instructions for each section thoroughly before starting. Understanding what is expected will help you approach the questions correctly.

- **Answer Every Question**: There is no penalty for guessing on the ASVAB, so answering every question is in your best interest. If you're unsure of an answer, make an educated guess rather than leaving it blank.

- **Stay Positive**: Maintain a positive attitude throughout the test. Confidence can significantly impact your performance, so believe in your preparation and abilities.

- **Pace Yourself**: Watch your time and pace yourself to ensure you can complete each section. Don't spend too much time on any one question.

.

7.2 Time Management Techniques

Time management is crucial when taking the ASVAB. Here are some techniques to help you manage your time effectively:

- **Set a Pace**: Determine how much time you can spend on each question. For example, if you have 30 minutes to complete 20 questions, aim to spend no more than 1.5 minutes per question.

- **Prioritize Questions**: Answer the easier questions first to secure those points, then return to the more challenging ones. This approach ensures you get as many correct answers as possible within the time limit.

- **Use a Timer**: Practice with a timer during your study sessions to simulate the test environment and improve your pacing.

- **Keep Moving**: If you encounter a difficult question, mark it and move on. Return to it after answering the easier questions to ensure you don't run out of time.

7.3 Answer Elimination Strategies

When you encounter a challenging question, use elimination strategies to narrow down your choices:

- **Rule Out Wrong Answers**: Eliminate any answer choices that are clearly incorrect. This increases your chances of selecting the correct answer from the remaining options.

- **Look for Clues**: Sometimes, the wording of the question or the other answer choices can provide hints about the correct answer. Pay attention to these clues.

- **Use Logic**: Apply logical reasoning to eliminate choices that don't make sense. Even if you don't know the exact answer, you can often use logic to rule out unlikely options.

- **Practice Process of Elimination**: Regularly practice using the process of elimination on sample questions. This will help you become more efficient at narrowing down your choices during the actual test.

7.4 Staying Calm and Focused

Staying calm and focused during the ASVAB is essential for performing well. Here are some techniques to help you maintain your composure:

- **Deep Breathing**: Practice deep breathing exercises to help reduce anxiety and maintain focus. Take slow, deep breaths in through your nose and out through your mouth.

- **Visualization**: Visualize yourself succeeding on the test. Positive visualization can boost your confidence and reduce stress.

- **Stay Present**: Focus on the present moment and the question in front of you. Avoid worrying about previous questions or future sections.

- **Take Breaks**: If allowed, take short breaks to stretch and relax between sections. This can help clear your mind and improve your focus for the next part of the test.

- **Mindfulness Techniques**: Incorporate mindfulness techniques into your daily routine to enhance your overall focus and stress management. Practices such as meditation can be very beneficial.

7.5 Day of the Test Tips

Preparation and strategy on the day of the test can significantly impact your performance. Here are some tips to help you succeed:

- **Get a Good Night's Sleep**: Ensure you get plenty of rest the night before the test. A well-rested mind performs better than a tired one.

- **Eat a Healthy Breakfast**: Have a nutritious breakfast to fuel your brain and body. Avoid heavy or greasy foods that can make you feel sluggish.

- **Arrive Early**: Plan to arrive at the test center early to give yourself plenty of time to check in and get settled. This can help reduce anxiety and allow you to start the test in a calm state of mind.

- **Bring Necessary Items**: Ensure you have all the required identification and materials for the test. Double-check the test center's requirements in advance.

- **Stay Hydrated**: Drink water before the test to stay hydrated. Dehydration can affect your concentration and cognitive function.

- **Review Key Concepts**: Briefly review key concepts and formulas before the test, but avoid cramming. Trust in your preparation and stay confident.

By applying these strategies and tips, you can enhance your test-taking skills and increase your chances of achieving a high score on the ASVAB. Consistent practice and a calm, focused approach will help you perform at your best on test day.

GET YOUR EXTRA CONTENTS NOW!

TO DOWNLOAD YOUR BONUS SCAN THE CODE BELOW

This bonus is 100% FREE, no strings attached

Or visit: https://rebrand.ly/615c65

ASVAB Study Guide

Chapter 8: Overcoming Challenges and Fears

8.1. Common Fears and Insecurities

Preparing for the ASVAB can bring up a range of fears and insecurities. Understanding these common concerns and learning how to address them can help you build confidence and approach the test with a positive mindset.

- **Fear of Failure**: Many candidates worry about not achieving a high enough score to qualify for their desired military role. This fear can create significant anxiety and hinder performance.

- **Test Anxiety**: Feeling nervous before and during the test is a common experience. Test anxiety can lead to difficulty concentrating, negative thoughts, and physical symptoms like sweating and a racing heart.

- **Doubting One's Abilities**: Self-doubt can undermine your preparation efforts and reduce your confidence. Doubting your ability to perform well on the ASVAB can be a significant obstacle to success.

- **Fear of the Unknown**: Uncertainty about the test format, types of questions, and overall testing experience can contribute to anxiety. Not knowing what to expect can make the test seem more daunting than it is.

- **Comparing Yourself to Others**: Comparing your progress and abilities to those of other candidates can increase stress and lead to feelings of inadequacy. It's important to focus on your own preparation and progress.

8.2 Building Confidence Through Preparation

Confidence comes from thorough preparation and a positive mindset. Here are some strategies to help you build confidence as you prepare for the ASVAB:

- **Set Realistic Goals**: Break down your study plan into manageable goals. Setting realistic, achievable goals can help you track your progress and build confidence over time.

- **Create a Study Schedule**: Establish a regular study routine that fits your lifestyle. Consistent, focused study sessions are more effective than last-minute cramming.

- **Use Practice Tests**: Take full-length practice tests to familiarize yourself with the test format and identify areas for improvement. Practice tests can also help you build stamina and reduce test anxiety.

- **Review Your Mistakes**: Carefully review the questions you get wrong on practice tests and understand why you made those mistakes. This will help you learn from them and avoid similar errors in the future.

- **Stay Positive**: Maintain a positive attitude throughout your preparation. Celebrate your achievements, no matter how small, and remind yourself of your progress.

- **Visualize Success**: Visualize yourself succeeding on the ASVAB. Positive visualization can boost your confidence and reduce anxiety.

8.3 Mindfulness and Stress Management Techniques

Managing stress and staying calm are crucial for performing well on the ASVAB. Incorporating mindfulness and stress management techniques into your routine can help you stay focused and relaxed.

- **Deep Breathing**: Practice deep breathing exercises to reduce anxiety and improve focus. Take slow, deep breaths in through your nose and out through your mouth to calm your mind and body.

- **Meditation**: Regular meditation can help you develop a calm, focused mindset. Even a few minutes of meditation each day can make a significant difference in your stress levels.

- **Progressive Muscle Relaxation**: This technique involves tensing and then relaxing each muscle group in your body. Progressive muscle relaxation can help reduce physical tension and promote relaxation.

- **Mindfulness Practices**: Incorporate mindfulness practices, such as mindful walking or mindful eating, into your daily routine. Mindfulness helps you stay present and reduces stress.

- **Exercise**: Regular physical activity can help reduce stress and improve your overall well-being. Exercise releases endorphins, which can boost your mood and energy levels.

- **Healthy Lifestyle**: Maintain a healthy lifestyle by eating nutritious foods, getting enough sleep, and staying hydrated. A healthy body supports a healthy mind.

8.4 Personal Stories: From Fear to Success

Hearing from others who have successfully navigated the ASVAB can provide inspiration and practical advice. Here are a few personal stories from individuals who overcame their fears and achieved success:

Story 1: Overcoming Test Anxiety

"Before taking the ASVAB, I was extremely nervous and doubted my abilities. I struggled with test anxiety and often second-guessed myself. However, I decided to create a structured study plan and stick to it. I took multiple practice tests and focused on understanding my mistakes. I also practiced deep breathing exercises to calm my nerves. On the day of the test, I felt prepared and confident. I passed with flying colors and qualified for my desired role in the Air Force. The key was consistent preparation and managing my anxiety." - Alex Z.

Story 2: Building Confidence Through Preparation

"I had always been an average student and never excelled in academics. When I decided to join the military, I was worried about the ASVAB. I started by setting small, achievable goals and gradually increased the difficulty of my study material. I used online resources, practice tests, and study guides to improve my knowledge. With each passing week, my confidence grew. By the time I took the ASVAB, I felt ready and scored higher than I ever expected. Consistent preparation and a positive attitude made all the difference." - Emily L.

Story 3: Facing the Fear of the Unknown

"As someone who had never taken a standardized test before, the ASVAB seemed intimidating. I was afraid of the unknown and didn't know where to start. I joined a study group with other candidates, and we shared resources and tips. The support and camaraderie helped me feel less alone in my journey. We practiced together, reviewed each other's work, and encouraged one another. On test day, I felt a sense of community and determination. I passed the ASVAB and found a great support network in my new military family." - Jake D.

Story 4: Megan From Doubt to Determination

"Self-doubt was my biggest obstacle. I often questioned my intelligence and capabilities. I decided to confront my doubts head-on by dedicating time each day to study and self-improvement. I read motivational books, listened to inspiring podcasts, and surrounded myself with positive influences. Gradually, my mindset shifted from doubt to determination. When I took the ASVAB, I approached it with a newfound sense of purpose. I exceeded my own expectations and realized that believing in myself was the first step to success." - Megan K.

Learn and Conquer: A Journey to Success

Imagine standing at the base of a mountain, looking up and wondering how you will reach the peak. The ASVAB might feel just as challenging, but success is not only for the smartest individuals – it's for those who are determined, prepared, and have the right mindset. Learning from personal stories and adopting proven strategies can transform your fears into stepping stones. Success on the ASVAB isn't just about intelligence; it's about perseverance, preparation, and a positive attitude. Think of yourself as a warrior, with focus as your shield, positivity as your sword, and belief in yourself as your armor.

Let these stories guide and motivate you. They can be powerful engines driving you toward victory. Stay focused, positive, and confident in succeeding in this exam. You've got this! It's remarkable how a good story can change your perspective. These success stories from past ASVAB candidates are blueprints for your own success. They demonstrate that the mountain can be climbed. Many have conquered the ASVAB through sheer determination. It's time to add your name to that list.

Consider these stories your personal cheerleaders. They remind you that others have faced similar challenges and prevailed. They provide you with knowledge and strategies. Preparation is essential. It's not just about cramming; it's about understanding the material, practicing regularly, and maintaining a positive attitude. Just like a marathon runner trains daily, you need consistent effort. Remember, Thomas Edison didn't invent the light bulb overnight. Your ASVAB journey is similar. Equip yourself with knowledge, stay focused, and believe in your success.

Feeling overwhelmed? Don't worry. Every challenge has its fears, but you are not alone. Thousands have walked this path, leaving behind valuable wisdom and strategies. Embrace these stories for motivation. Are you ready to conquer the ASVAB? With determination, preparation, and the right mindset, you are on your way. Stay positive, keep your eyes on the prize, and remember – you've got this. Go ahead, conquer that mountain. The summit awaits you.

Take your preparation to the next level with our exclusive bonus content!

Download the **2500+ Q&A Explained** for comprehensive practice and detailed explanations. This invaluable resource will help you understand the reasoning behind each answer, ensuring you grasp the concepts and are fully prepared for every section of the ASVAB.

Don't miss out on this essential tool—scan the QR code below to download now and maximize your study efforts!

GET YOUR EXTRA CONTENTS NOW!

TO DOWNLOAD YOUR BONUS SCAN THE CODE BELOW

This bonus is 100% FREE, no strings attached

Or visit https://rebrand.ly/615c65

Chapter 9: Practice Exams and Mock Tests

To help you prepare effectively for the ASVAB, we have included two full-length practice tests. These tests are designed to simulate the actual exam conditions and provide a comprehensive review of all the topics covered in the ASVAB. Each section mimics the official ASVAB test in terms of question format and timing. The practice test should be taken in a quiet environment, and the user should adhere strictly to the time limits for each section to simulate the actual testing conditions.

General Structure of an ASVAB Full-Length Practice Test

Sections and Timing

Section	Number of Questions	Time	Content
General Science (GS)	25	8 minutes	Covers basic concepts in physical and biological sciences.
Arithmetic Reasoning (AR)	30	36 minutes	Focuses on solving basic arithmetic problems encountered in everyday life.
Word Knowledge (WK)	35	11 minutes	Tests the ability to understand the meaning of words through synonyms and antonyms.
Paragraph Comprehension (PC)	15	13 minutes	Measures the ability to obtain information from written material.
Mathematics Knowledge (MK)	25	24 minutes	Tests knowledge of mathematical concepts and applications, including algebra and geometry.
Electronics Information (EI)	20	9 minutes	Covers basic electronic principles and concepts.
Auto and Shop Information (AS)	25	11 minutes	Assesses knowledge of automotive maintenance and repair, and wood and metal shop practices.
Mechanical Comprehension (MC)	25	19 minutes	Tests understanding of mechanical and physical principles.
Assembling Objects (AO)	25	17 minutes	Measures spatial relationship skills through visualizing how objects fit together.

Instructions

- **Find a Quiet Environment**: Choose a distraction-free space to take the test.
- **Set a Timer**: Adhere to the time limits for each section of the ASVAB.
- **Avoid External Resources**: Answer every question to the best of your ability without using any external aids.

Test Simulation: Complete the practice test in one sitting, just as you would during the actual ASVAB. This will help you build stamina and get accustomed to the test format.

Start with the first full-length practice test to assess your current level of knowledge and identify areas where you need to improve.

After completing the first practice test, use the answer key to check your responses. Review the explanations for each question to understand why the correct answers are right and why the incorrect answers are wrong. This step is crucial for learning from your mistakes and improving your understanding of the material.

Important Note: Don't miss the opportunity to enhance your study experience—scan the QR code to download 2500 practice questions and answers explained in detail, completely free! Practicing with as many tests as possible is one of the keys to scoring high on the exam.

GET YOUR EXTRA CONTENTS NOW!

TO DOWNLOAD YOUR BONUS SCAN THE CODE BELOW

This bonus is 100% FREE, no strings attached

9.1. Full-Length Practice Test

General Science (GS)

Question 1: What is the primary function of the mitochondria in a cell?

A. Protein synthesis

B. Photosynthesis

C. Energy production

D. DNA replication

Question 2: Which of the following elements is essential for the process of photosynthesis in plants?

A. Nitrogen

B. Oxygen

C. Carbon dioxide

D. Hydrogen

Question 3: What is the chemical formula for table salt?

A. NaCl

B. H2O

C. CO2

D. C6H12O6

Question 4: What is the most abundant gas in the Earth's atmosphere?

A. Oxygen

B. Nitrogen

C. Carbon dioxide

D. Hydrogen

Question 5: Which part of the cell is responsible for controlling cell activities and contains DNA?

A. Nucleus

B. Cytoplasm

C. Ribosome

D. Cell membrane

Question 6: In what part of the human body would you find the femur?

A. Arm

B. Leg

C. Skull

D. Chest

Question 7: Which of the following processes is used by green plants to convert sunlight into chemical energy?

A. Digestion

B. Respiration

C. Photosynthesis

D. Fermentation

Question 8: What type of bond involves the sharing of electron pairs between atoms?

A. Ionic bond

B. Covalent bond

C. Hydrogen bond

D. Metallic bond

Question 9: Which organ in the human body is primarily responsible for filtering and removing waste products from the blood?

A. Heart

B. Liver

C. Kidney

D. Lung

Question 10: What is the pH value of a neutral substance, like pure water?

    A. 0

    B. 7

    C. 14

    D. 1

Question 11: Which planet is known as the "Red Planet"?

    A. Venus

    B. Mars

    C. Jupiter

    D. Saturn

Question 12: What is the primary source of energy for the Earth's climate system?

    A. The moon

    B. Geothermal energy

    C. The sun

    D. Ocean currents

Question 13: Which of the following is a renewable resource?

    A. Coal

    B. Natural gas

    C. Solar energy

    D. Petroleum

Question 14: What type of rock is formed from the cooling and solidification of magma or lava?

    A. Sedimentary

    B. Metamorphic

    C. Igneous

    D. Fossil

Question 15: Which part of the plant is primarily responsible for water absorption?

    A. Stem

    B. Leaf

    C. Flower

    D. Root

Question 16: What is the basic unit of life?

    A. Atom

    B. Molecule

    C. Cell

    D. Tissue

Question 17: What is the boiling point of water at sea level?

    A. 90°C

    B. 95°C

    C. 100°C

    D. 105°C

Question 18: Which planet is closest to the Sun?

    A. Venus

    B. Earth

    C. Mercury

    D. Mars

Question 19: What is the chemical formula for carbon dioxide?

    A. CO

    B. CO_2

    C. C_2O

    D. C_2O_2

Question 20: What part of the cell contains the genetic material?

    A. Cytoplasm

    B. Nucleus

    C. Cell membrane

    D. Ribosome

Question 21: Which organ in the human body is primarily responsible for filtering blood?

    A. Liver

    B. Kidney

    C. Heart

    D. Lungs

Question 22: What type of rock is formed from the cooling and solidification of magma or lava?

    A. Sedimentary

    B. Metamorphic

    C. Igneous

    D. Fossil

Question 23: What is the powerhouse of the cell?

    A. Nucleus

    B. Ribosome

    C. Mitochondria

    D. Endoplasmic reticulum

Question 24: Which gas is most abundant in the Earth's atmosphere?

    A. Oxygen

    B. Nitrogen

    C. Carbon dioxide

    D. Hydrogen

Question 25: What is the primary function of red blood cells?

A. Fight infection

B. Clot blood

C. Carry oxygen

D. Produce hormones

Arithmetic Reasoning (AR)

Question 26: If a car travels 240 miles in 4 hours, what is the average speed of the car in miles per hour?

A. 40 mph

B. 50 mph

C. 60 mph

D. 70 mph

Question 27: John bought 3 pencils at $0.75 each and 2 notebooks at $1.25 each. How much did John spend in total?

A. $3.75

B. $4.25

C. $4.75

D. $5.00

Question 28: If a worker earns $15 per hour and works 40 hours a week, what is his weekly income?

A. $500

B. $600

C. $700

D. $800

Question 29: A train travels 150 miles in 2.5 hours. What is its average speed in miles per hour?

    A. 50 mph

    B. 55 mph

    C. 60 mph

    D. 65 mph

Question 30: If a recipe calls for 2/3 cup of sugar and you want to make half of the recipe, how much sugar do you need?

    A. 1/6 cup

    B. 1/3 cup

    C. 1/2 cup

    D. 2/3 cup

Question 31: Sarah bought 4 bags of apples. Each bag contains 6 apples. If she wants to distribute the apples equally among 3 friends, how many apples will each friend get?

    A. 6

    B. 8

    C. 10

    D. 12

Question 32: If a jacket is discounted by 20% and its sale price is $80, what was the original price?

    A. $90

    B. $95

    C. $100

    D. $105

Question 33: A store sells oranges at 3 for $1. How much will 15 oranges cost?

    A. $3

    B. $4

    C. $5

    D. $6

Question 34: Tom had $50. He spent $18.75 on a book and $12.50 on lunch. How much money does he have left?

    A. $18.75
    B. $19.25
    C. $20.00
    D. $21.25

Question 35: If a man buys 4 shirts at $12 each and gets a 10% discount on the total purchase, how much does he pay?

    A. $40.80
    B. $43.20
    C. $46.00
    D. $48.00

Question 36: A farmer has 15 cows and 10 pigs. What is the ratio of pigs to cows?

    A. 1:2
    B. 2:3
    C. 2:1
    D. 3:2

Question 37: If 5 workers can complete a job in 8 hours, how many hours will it take 10 workers to complete the same job, assuming they work at the same rate?

    A. 2 hours
    B. 4 hours
    C. 6 hours
    D. 8 hours

Question 38: A student scored 85, 90, 78, and 92 on four tests. What is the student's average score?

    A. 85
    B. 86.25
    C. 87.5
    D. 88.75

Question 39: A tank holds 500 gallons of water. If it is filled at a rate of 25 gallons per minute, how long will it take to fill the tank?

    A. 10 minutes

    B. 15 minutes

    C. 20 minutes

    D. 25 minutes

Question 40: If the price of a laptop is $800 and it is increased by 15%, what is the new price?

    A. $880

    B. $900

    C. $920

    D. $960

Question 41: A car uses 12 gallons of gas to travel 300 miles. What is the car's fuel efficiency in miles per gallon?

    A. 20 mpg

    B. 25 mpg

    C. 30 mpg

    D. 35 mpg

Question 42: If the ratio of boys to girls in a class is 3:4 and there are 24 girls, how many boys are there?

    A. 12

    B. 18

    C. 21

    D. 24

Question 43: A phone is discounted by 25% and its sale price is $300. What was the original price?

    A. $350

    B. $375

    C. $400

    D. $450

Question 44: A rectangle has a length of 10 meters and a width of 6 meters. What is its perimeter?

A. 16 meters

B. 20 meters

C. 26 meters

D. 32 meters

Question 45: If a bag contains 3 red balls, 2 blue balls, and 5 green balls, what is the probability of drawing a red ball?

A. 1/10

B. 1/5

C. 3/10

D. 3/5

Question 46: If you buy 3 books at $8 each and a pen for $2, how much do you spend in total?

A. $24

B. $25

C. $26

D. $27

Question 47: A man buys a suit for $150, a shirt for $30, and a tie for $20. If he gets a 10% discount on the total purchase, how much does he pay?

A. $180

B. $180.50

C. $180.80

D. $180.90

Question 48: If a garden is 15 meters long and 10 meters wide, what is the area of the garden?

A. 100 square meters

B. 120 square meters

C. 130 square meters

D. 150 square meters

Question 49: If you invest $500 at an interest rate of 5% per year, how much interest will you earn in one year?

    A. $20

    B. $25

    C. $30

    D. $35

Question 50: A school has 500 students, and 60% of them are girls. How many girls are there in the school?

    A. 200

    B. 250

    C. 300

    D. 350

Question 51: If a car rental company charges $20 per day and $0.10 per mile, how much will it cost to rent a car for 3 days and drive it 150 miles?

    A. $45

    B. $50

    C. $55

    D. $60

Question 52: If a shirt costs $25 and is marked down by 20%, what is the sale price of the shirt?

    A. $15

    B. $18

    C. $20

    D. $22

Question 53: If a car's fuel efficiency is 30 miles per gallon, how many gallons of gas are needed to travel 450 miles?

    A. 10 gallons

    B. 12 gallons

    C. 15 gallons

    D. 18 gallons

Question 54: A phone is originally priced at $600 and is on sale for 25% off. What is the sale price?

    A. $400

    B. $450

    C. $475

    D. $500

Question 55: If a cake recipe requires 3/4 cup of sugar and you want to make 1/2 of the recipe, how much sugar do you need?

    A. 1/8 cup

    B. 1/4 cup

    C. 3/8 cup

    D. 1/2 cup

Word Knowledge (WK)

Question 56: The word "gregarious" most nearly means:

    A. Shy

    B. Friendly

    C. Sad

    D. Angry

Question 57: The word "prudent" most nearly means:

    A. Reckless

    B. Stupid

    C. Careful

    D. Brave

Question 58: The word "obsolete" most nearly means:

    A. New

    B. Useful

    C. Outdated

    D. Expensive

Question 59: The word "verbose" most nearly means:

    A. Quiet

    B. Talkative

    C. Rude

    D. Angry

Question 60: The word "benevolent" most nearly means:

    A. Malevolent

    B. Kind

    C. Angry

    D. Lazy

Question 61: The word "coerce" most nearly means:

    A. Persuade

    B. Liberate

    C. Compel

    D. Ignore

Question 62: The word "diligent" most nearly means:

    A. Lazy

    B. Hardworking

    C. Careless

    D. Intelligent

Question 63: The word "mitigate" most nearly means:

    A. Aggravate

    B. Increase

    C. Lessen

    D. Ignore

Question 64: The word "candid" most nearly means:

    A. Deceptive

    B. Honest

    C. Indirect

    D. Secretive

Question 65: The word "emulate" most nearly means:

    A. Avoid

    B. Imitate

    C. Disregard

    D. Condemn

Question 66: The word "lucid" most nearly means:

    A. Confused

    B. Clear

    C. Dull

    D. Dark

Question 67: The word "animosity" most nearly means:

    A. Friendship

    B. Hostility

    C. Indifference

    D. Sympathy

Question 68: The word "arduous" most nearly means:

    A. Easy

    B. Difficult

    C. Boring

    D. Quick

Question 69: The word "ostentatious" most nearly means:

    A. Humble

    B. Showy

    C. Plain

    D. Reserved

Question 70: The word "placate" most nearly means:

    A. Agitate

    B. Soothe

    C. Ignore

    D. Challenge

Question 71: The word "prolific" most nearly means:

    A. Unproductive

    B. Fruitful

    C. Rare

    D. Diminishing

Question 72: The word "vindicate" most nearly means:

    A. Accuse

    B. Justify

    C. Ignore

    D. Conceal

Question 73: The word "adamant" most nearly means:

    A. Flexible

    B. Yielding

    C. Unyielding

    D. Indecisive

Question 74: The word "nefarious" most nearly means:

    A. Kind

    B. Wicked

    C. Honest

    D. Generous

Question 75: The word "ephemeral" most nearly means:

    A. Lasting

    B. Permanent

    C. Brief

    D. Tedious

Question 76: The word "frugal" most nearly means:

    A. Wasteful

    B. Generous

    C. Thrifty

    D. Extravagant

Question 77: The word "ardent" most nearly means:

    A. Indifferent

    B. Passionate

    C. Distant

    D. Cold

Question 78: The word "malleable" most nearly means:

    A. Rigid

    B. Flexible

    C. Brittle

    D. Hard

Question 79: The word "altruistic" most nearly means:

A. Selfish

B. Generous

C. Greedy

D. Stingy

Question 80: The word "copious" most nearly means:

A. Scarce

B. Abundant

C. Minimal

D. Insufficient

Question 81: The word "elusive" most nearly means:

A. Visible

B. Clear

C. Evasive

D. Apparent

Question 82: The word "callous" most nearly means:

A. Sensitive

B. Compassionate

C. Unfeeling

D. Caring

Question 83: The word "tenacious" most nearly means:

A. Weak

B. Persistent

C. Reluctant

D. Hesitant

Question 84: The word "gregarious" most nearly means:

    A. Sociable

    B. Reserved

    C. Silent

    D. Unfriendly

Question 85: The word "perfunctory" most nearly means:

    A. Thorough

    B. Careless

    C. Detailed

    D. Diligent

Question 86: The word "ubiquitous" most nearly means:

    A. Rare

    B. Omnipresent

    C. Hidden

    D. Uncommon

Question 87: The word "laconic" most nearly means:

    A. Verbose

    B. Quiet

    C. Talkative

    D. Reserved

Question 88: The word "innate" most nearly means:

    A. Acquired

    B. Inborn

    C. Learned

    D. External

Question 89: The word "zealous" most nearly means:

A. Apathetic

B. Enthusiastic

C. Indifferent

D. Uninterested

Question 90: The word "succinct" most nearly means:

A. Verbose

B. Concise

C. Detailed

D. Lengthy

Paragraph Comprehension (PC)

Question 91: Passage: The rapid advancement of technology has significantly transformed the workplace. Automation and artificial intelligence have streamlined many processes, increasing efficiency and reducing the need for manual labor.

Question: What can be inferred about the impact of technology on jobs?

A. Technology has made all jobs easier.

B. Technology has eliminated the need for all jobs.

C. Technology has increased the need for manual labor.

D. Technology has reduced the need for some manual labor jobs.

Question 92: Passage: The serene lake was a stark contrast to the bustling city. The calm waters and gentle breeze provided a peaceful escape from the noise and chaos of urban life.

Question: The word "serene" most nearly means:

A. Calm

B. Noisy

C. Busy

D. Dirty

Question 93: Passage: The Great Wall of China was built to protect against invasions. It stretches over 13,000 miles and is one of the most impressive architectural feats in history.

Question: What is the primary purpose of the Great Wall of China?

A. To attract tourists

B. To protect against invasions

C. To serve as a trade route

D. To display architectural skills

Question 94: Passage: Many people are turning to renewable energy sources, such as solar and wind power, to reduce their carbon footprint and combat climate change.

Question: According to the passage, why are people turning to renewable energy sources?

A. To save money

B. To reduce their carbon footprint

C. To increase energy consumption

D. To avoid using electricity

Question 95: Passage: The Amazon Rainforest, often referred to as the "lungs of the Earth," plays a critical role in regulating the planet's climate by absorbing large amounts of carbon dioxide.

Question: Why is the Amazon Rainforest referred to as the "lungs of the Earth"?

A. It produces a large amount of oxygen

B. It is the largest forest in the world

C. It absorbs large amounts of carbon dioxide

D. It has a diverse range of species

Question 96: Passage: Regular exercise has numerous health benefits, including improving cardiovascular health, strengthening muscles, and enhancing mental well-being.

Question: According to the passage, which of the following is NOT a benefit of regular exercise?

A. Improving cardiovascular health

B. Strengthening muscles

C. Enhancing mental well-being

D. Increasing appetite

Question 97: Passage: The invention of the internet has revolutionized communication, allowing people to connect instantly across the globe and access a vast amount of information.

Question: What is one impact of the invention of the internet mentioned in the passage?

A. Decreasing the speed of communication
B. Limiting access to information
C. Allowing instant global connections
D. Reducing the number of books read

Question 98: Passage: During the Renaissance, there was a renewed interest in art, science, and literature, leading to significant cultural and intellectual advancements.

Question: What was one result of the Renaissance mentioned in the passage?

A. Decline in scientific discoveries
B. Cultural and intellectual advancements
C. Decreased interest in literature
D. Stagnation in artistic expression

Question 99: Passage: The primary function of leaves is to carry out photosynthesis, a process that converts sunlight into chemical energy for the plant.

Question: What is the main role of leaves according to the passage?

A. To provide shade
B. To absorb water
C. To carry out photosynthesis
D. To protect the plant

Question 100: Passage: In order to preserve the historical site, visitors are required to follow strict guidelines, including not touching the artifacts and staying on designated paths.

Question: What is one guideline mentioned in the passage that visitors must follow to preserve the historical site?

A. Taking photos
B. Touching the artifacts
C. Staying on designated paths
D. Collecting souvenirs

Question 101: Passage: The primary goal of the new educational program is to enhance students' critical thinking skills and prepare them for future challenges.

Question: What is the main objective of the new educational program mentioned in the passage?

A. To reduce homework

B. To improve critical thinking skills

C. To increase school attendance

D. To provide free meals

Question 102: Passage: Despite the challenging economic conditions, the company managed to increase its revenue by focusing on innovation and customer satisfaction.

Question: According to the passage, what strategy did the company use to increase its revenue?

- A. Reducing prices
- B. Expanding globally
- C. Focusing on innovation and customer satisfaction
- D. Cutting employee benefits

Question 103: Passage: The architect designed the building with sustainability in mind, incorporating energy-efficient systems and environmentally friendly materials.

Question: What was one consideration the architect had when designing the building?

A. Cost reduction

B. Aesthetics

C. Sustainability

D. Historical accuracy

Question 104: Passage: The new policy aims to reduce traffic congestion by encouraging the use of public transportation and carpooling.

Question: What is the main goal of the new policy according to the passage?

A. To build more roads

B. To reduce traffic congestion

C. To increase vehicle sales

D. To decrease fuel prices

Question 105: Passage: The scientist's groundbreaking research provided new insights into the causes of climate change and offered potential solutions to mitigate its effects.

Question: What did the scientist's research focus on according to the passage?

A. Advancing medical technology

B. Understanding climate change

C. Developing new communication tools

D. Improving agricultural practices

Mathematics Knowledge (MK) 25

Question 106: What is the area of a rectangle with a length of 8 meters and a width of 5 meters?

A. 13 square meters

B. 30 square meters

C. 40 square meters

D. 45 square meters

Question 107: *If $x = 4$ and $y = 2$,* what is the value of $3x + 2y$?

A. 10

B. 12

C. 14

D. 16

Question 108: What is the solution to the equation $2x - 3 = 7$?

A. 2

B. 3

C. 5

D. 6

Question 109: What is the volume of a cube with a side length of 3 cm?

    A. 9 cubic cm

    B. 18 cubic cm

    C. 27 cubic cm

    D. 36 cubic cm

Question 110: Simplify the expression 4(3x−5)

    A. 12x - 5

    B. 12x - 20

    C. 7x - 5

    D. 7x - 20

Question 111: $If\,(a = 6)\,and\,(b = 2),\,what\;is\;the\;value\;of\,(\frac{a^2}{b})?$

    A. 12

    B. 18

    C. 24

    D. 36

Question 112: $Solve\;for\;y\;in\;the\;equation\;3y + 4 = 19$

    A. 3

    B. 4

    C. 5

    D. 6

Question 113: What is the hypotenuse of a right triangle with legs of 6 cm and 8 cm?

    A. 10 cm

    B. 12 cm

    C. 14 cm

    D. 16 cm

Question 114: What is 15% of 200?

    A. 20

    B. 25

    C. 30

    D. 35

Question 115: If $x = -3$x, what is the value of $x^2 - 4x + 5$?

    A. 10

    B. 14

    C. 20

    D. 26

Question 116: What is the slope of the line passing through the points (2, 3) and (5, 11)?

    A. 2

    B. 2.5

    C. 3

    D. 3.5

Question 117: Simplify the expression $\frac{2x^2 - 8x}{2x}$.

    A. x−4

    B. x−2

    C. x+4

    D. x+2

Question 118: Convert 3.5% to a decimal.

    A. 0.35

    B. 0.035

    C. 0.0035

    D. 0.35

Question 119: What is the solution to the equation $5x - 2 = 3x + 8$

    A. 2

    B. 3

    C. 4

    D. 5

Question 120: Find the perimeter of a triangle with sides of lengths 7 cm, 9 cm, and 12 cm.

    A. 24 cm

    B. 28 cm

    C. 30 cm

    D. 32 cm

Question 121: Simplify the expression $(3x^2y)(4xy^2)$

    A. $12x^3y^2$

    B. $12x^3y^3$

    C. $12x^2y^2$

    D. $12x^2y^3$

Question 122: If the area of a circle is 16π square cm, what is the radius of the circle?

    A. 2 cm

    B. 3 cm

    C. 4 cm

    D. 5 cm

Question 123: Solve for z: $4z-7=13$.

    A. 3

    B. 4

    C. 5

    D. 6

Question 124: What is the value of 5!(5 factorial)?

    A. 20

    B. 60

    C. 100

    D. 120

Question 125: *If $(x + 2 = 7)$, what is the value of $(2x + 1)$?*

    A. 7

    B. 9

    C. 11

    D. 13

Question 126: What is the midpoint of the line segment with endpoints (2, 3) and (8, 11)?

    A. (3, 4)

    B. (4, 5)

    C. (5, 7)

    D. (6, 8)

Question 127: Solve for y: $2y + 3 = 9$

    A. 2

    B. 3

    C. 4

    D. 5

Question 128: If the perimeter of a square is 24 cm, what is the length of one side?

    A. 4 cm

    B. 5 cm

    C. 6 cm

    D. 7 cm

Question 129: What is 8×10^{-3} as a decimal?

A. 0.08

B. 0.008

C. 0.0008

D. 0.00008

Question 130: *If* $(x = 3)$ *and* $(y = 4)$, *what is the value of* $(x^2 + y^2)$?

A. 16

B. 17

C. 24

D. 25

Electronics Information (EI)

Question 131: What is the unit of electric current?

A. Volt

B. Ohm

C. Ampere

D. Watt

Question 132: Which of the following components stores electrical energy in an electric field?

A. Resistor

B. Capacitor

C. Inductor

D. Transformer

Question 133: What type of current is supplied by a typical household electrical outlet in the United States?

A. Direct current (DC)

B. Alternating current (AC)

C. Pulsating current

D. Static current

Question 134: What is the function of a diode in an electronic circuit?

    A. To store charge

    B. To resist current

    C. To allow current to flow in only one direction

    D. To amplify signals

Question 135: Which component is used to step up or step down AC voltage levels?

    A. Capacitor

    B. Resistor

    C. Transistor

    D. Transformer

Question 136: What is the purpose of a fuse in an electrical circuit?

    A. To store energy

    B. To provide a path for current

    C. To protect the circuit by breaking the connection in case of an overload

    D. To convert AC to DC

Question 137: What does LED stand for?

    A. Light Emitting Diode

    B. Light Energy Device

    C. Low Emission Diode

    D. Low Energy Device

Question 138: In a simple electrical circuit, if the voltage is 12 volts and the resistance is 6 ohms, what is the current?

    A. 1 ampere

    B. 2 amperes

    C. 3 amperes

    D. 4 amperes

Question 139: What type of semiconductor device is used to amplify or switch electronic signals?

    A. Capacitor

    B. Inductor

    C. Resistor

    D. Transistor

Question 140: Which of the following is a common use for a potentiometer?

    A. To measure current

    B. To adjust voltage

    C. To store charge

    D. To convert AC to DC

Question 141: What is the purpose of an inductor in an electronic circuit?

    A. To resist current

    B. To store energy in a magnetic field

    C. To convert AC to DC

    D. To amplify signals

Question 142: Which device is used to measure electrical resistance?

    A. Voltmeter

    B. Ammeter

    C. Ohmmeter

    D. Oscilloscope

Question 143: What is the main advantage of using a transistor over a vacuum tube in electronic devices?

    A. Larger size

    B. Higher power consumption

    C. Faster switching speed

    D. Higher heat generation

Question 144: What is the primary function of a resistor in an electronic circuit?

    A. To amplify signals

    B. To convert AC to DC

    C. To limit current

    D. To store energy

Question 145: Which of the following symbols represents a resistor in a circuit diagram?

    A. Zigzag line

    B. Straight line

    C. Circle

    D. Triangle

Question 146: What is the typical voltage of a standard AA battery?

    A. 1.2 volts

    B. 1.5 volts

    C. 3.0 volts

    D. 9.0 volts

Question 147: In an electrical circuit, what is the function of a switch?

    A. To amplify current

    B. To store electrical energy

    C. To open or close the circuit

    D. To convert AC to DC

Question 148: What does the term "ground" refer to in electronics?

    A. A component that stores energy

    B. A point of reference for voltage levels

    C. A device that amplifies signals

    D. A type of resistor

Question 149: What is the main purpose of a rectifier in an electronic circuit?

A. To amplify signals

B. To convert AC to DC

C. To measure resistance

D. To store energy

Question 150: Which component is used to protect electronic circuits from excessive current?

A. Capacitor

B. Resistor

C. Fuse

D. Inductor

Auto and Shop Information (AS)

Question 151: What tool is commonly used to drive nails into wood?

A. Screwdriver

B. Wrench

C. Hammer

D. Pliers

Question 152: Which part of the car is responsible for cooling the engine?

A. Radiator

B. Alternator

C. Carburetor

D. Distributor

Question 153: What does the alternator do in a vehicle?

A. Provides spark to the engine

B. Charges the battery and powers the electrical system when the engine is running

C. Controls the fuel injection system

D. Filters the engine oil

Question 154: Which tool is used to measure the internal diameter of a cylinder?

    A. Vernier caliper

    B. Micrometer

    C. Feeler gauge

    D. Dial bore gauge

Question 155: What is the function of a torque wrench?

    A. To measure the force applied to a fastener

    B. To cut metal

    C. To drill holes

    D. To sand surfaces

Question 156: In automotive terms, what does the abbreviation "EFI" stand for?

    A. Electronic Fuel Injection

    B. Electrical Function Indicator

    C. Engine Fuel Indicator

    D. Emergency Fuel Injector

Question 157: Which type of saw is most commonly used for cutting curves in wood?

    A. Table saw

    B. Circular saw

    C. Jigsaw

    D. Miter saw

Question 158: What automotive system uses a catalytic converter?

    A. Electrical system

    B. Exhaust system

    C. Cooling system

    D. Brake system

Question 159: What is the purpose of engine oil?

    A. To cool the engine

    B. To lubricate engine parts

    C. To power the fuel injectors

    D. To clean the air filter

Question 160: Which tool is used to check the gap in a spark plug?

    A. Torque wrench

    B. Feeler gauge

    C. Micrometer

    D. Vernier caliper

Question 161: What material is commonly used for brake pads?

    A. Wood

    B. Plastic

    C. Ceramic

    D. Glass

Question 162: Which part of the engine converts linear motion into rotational motion?

    A. Crankshaft

    B. Piston

    C. Camshaft

    D. Flywheel

Question 163: Which tool is used to remove the insulation from electrical wires?

    A. Wire stripper

    B. Pliers

    C. Screwdriver

    D. Wrench

Question 164: What is the purpose of a muffler in a vehicle?

A. To increase engine power

B. To reduce exhaust noise

C. To filter the air intake

D. To cool the engine

Question 165: What type of joint is created by welding?

A. Adhesive joint

B. Mechanical joint

C. Fusion joint

D. Threaded joint

Question 166: Which tool is commonly used to shape metal by hammering?

A. Lathe

B. Anvil

C. Drill press

D. Grinder

Question 167: What is the main purpose of coolant in a vehicle's engine?

A. To lubricate the engine

B. To reduce friction

C. To regulate the engine temperature

D. To clean the fuel injectors

Question 168: What tool is used to create threads on the inside of a hole?

A. Tap

B. Die

C. Reamer

D. Lathe

Question 169: Which part of a vehicle's suspension system absorbs and dampens shocks from the road?

    A. Axle

    B. Shock absorber

    C. Driveshaft

    D. Differential

Question 170: Which type of file is used for sharpening saw blades?

    A. Mill file

    B. Round file

    C. Triangular file

    D. Flat file

Question 171: In an automobile, what is the function of the clutch?

    A. To start the engine

    B. To change gears

    C. To apply the brakes

    D. To provide power to the wheels

Question 172: Which type of wrench is used to turn hex and square bolts?

    A. Pipe wrench

    B. Box-end wrench

    C. Adjustable wrench

    D. Allen wrench

Question 173: What is the purpose of sandpaper in woodworking?

    A. To cut wood

    B. To join wood pieces

    C. To smooth and finish wood surfaces

    D. To measure wood thickness

Question 174: Which component in an engine controls the opening and closing of the valves?

    A. Crankshaft

    B. Camshaft

    C. Flywheel

    D. Piston

Question 175: What is the purpose of a planer in woodworking?

    A. To drill holes

    B. To smooth and flatten wood surfaces

    C. To cut intricate shapes

    D. To join wood pieces

Mechanical Comprehension (MC)

Question 176: Which simple machine consists of a wheel with a rope or cable around it?

    A. Lever

    B. Pulley

    C. Inclined plane

    D. Screw

Question 177: What is the mechanical advantage of a lever with an effort arm of 4 meters and a resistance arm of 1 meter?

    A. 1

    B. 2

    C. 3

    D. 4

Question 178: What is the purpose of a hydraulic jack?

    A. To cut metal

    B. To lift heavy objects

    C. To generate electricity

    D. To measure pressure

Question 179: Which principle explains why ships float?

    A. Bernoulli's principle

    B. Pascal's principle

    C. Archimedes' principle

    D. Newton's third law

Question 180: What type of gear is used to change the direction of rotational motion by 90 degrees?

    A. Spur gear

    B. Bevel gear

    C. Helical gear

    D. Worm gear

Question 181: What is the function of a flywheel in an engine?

    A. To store rotational energy

    B. To cool the engine

    C. To increase fuel efficiency

    D. To measure engine speed

Question 182: What is the primary purpose of a ball bearing?

    A. To reduce friction

    B. To increase speed

    C. To generate power

    D. To provide cushioning

Question 183: If a machine has an input force of 50 N and an output force of 200 N, what is its mechanical advantage?

A. 2

B. 3

C. 4

D. 5

Question 184: Which type of simple machine is a ramp?

A. Lever

B. Wedge

C. Inclined plane

D. Pulley

Question 185: What is the function of a brake drum in an automotive braking system?

A. To increase engine power

B. To stop the vehicle by creating friction

C. To cool the engine

D. To measure speed

Question 186: In a hydraulic system, what is the purpose of the fluid?

A. To lubricate moving parts

B. To cool the system

C. To transfer force

D. To measure pressure

Question 187: Which law states that for every action, there is an equal and opposite reaction?

A. Newton's first law

B. Newton's second law

C. Newton's third law

D. Archimedes' principle

Question 188: What type of motion does a camshaft convert?

    A. Linear motion to rotational motion

    B. Rotational motion to linear motion

    C. Linear motion to angular motion

    D. Rotational motion to angular motion

Question 189: If a pulley system has four supporting ropes, what is the mechanical advantage of the system?

    A. 1

    B. 2

    C. 3

    D. 4

Question 190: What is the unit of measurement for power in the International System of Units (SI)?

    A. Joule

    B. Newton

    C. Watt

    D. Pascal

Question 191: What is the purpose of a gear ratio in a mechanical system?

    A. To increase friction

    B. To decrease torque

    C. To change the speed and torque

    D. To measure force

Question 192: Which of the following is a characteristic of a first-class lever?

    A. The fulcrum is located between the effort and the load

    B. The load is located between the effort and the fulcrum

    C. The effort is located between the load and the fulcrum

    D. The fulcrum is at one end, and the effort is applied at the other end

Question 193: What type of machine is a bicycle wheel and axle?

    A. Lever

    B. Pulley

    C. Inclined plane

    D. Wheel and axle

Question 194: What is the purpose of a fuse in an electrical circuit?

    A. To store electrical energy

    B. To measure electrical current

    C. To protect the circuit by breaking the connection if the current is too high

    D. To amplify the electrical signal

Question 195: Which component in an internal combustion engine converts chemical energy into mechanical energy?

    A. Crankshaft

    B. Piston

    C. Cylinder head

    D. Spark plug

Question 196: What is the purpose of a spring in a mechanical system?

    A. To increase speed

    B. To store and release energy

    C. To reduce friction

    D. To generate power

Question 197: In a screw jack, what type of simple machine is the screw considered?

    A. Lever

    B. Pulley

    C. Inclined plane

    D. Wedge

Question 198: What is the main advantage of using a compound pulley system over a single pulley?

    A. Increased speed

    B. Decreased weight

    C. Increased mechanical advantage

    D. Decreased friction

Question 199: Which principle states that the pressure in a fluid decreases as the fluid's velocity increases?

    A. Pascal's principle

    B. Archimedes' principle

    C. Newton's second law

    D. Bernoulli's principle

Question 200: Which type of mechanical linkage converts rotational motion into reciprocating motion?

    A. Crankshaft

    B. Camshaft

    C. Gearbox

    D. Differential

Assembling Objects (AO)

Question 201: Which of these images best shows how to assemble the parts shown in the first picture?

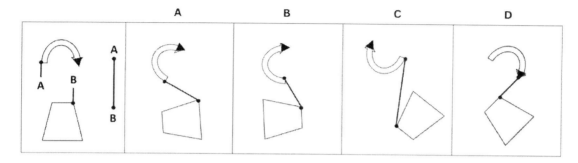

- A
- B
- C
- D

Question 202: Which of these images best shows how to assemble the parts shown in the first picture?

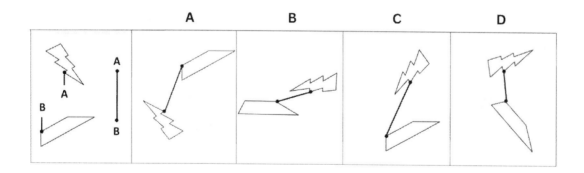

- A
- B
- C
- D

Question 203: Which of these images best shows how to assemble the parts shown in the first picture?

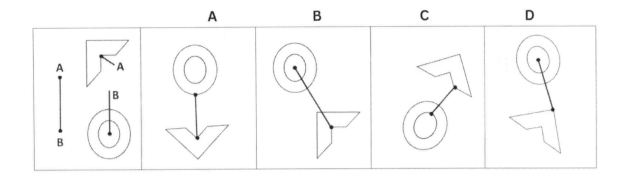

- A
- B
- C
- D

Question 204: Which of these images best shows how to assemble the parts shown in the first picture?

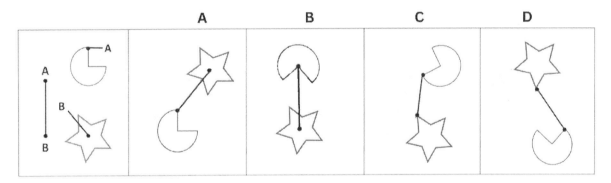

- A
- B
- C
- D

Question 205: Which of these images best shows how to assemble the parts shown in the first picture?

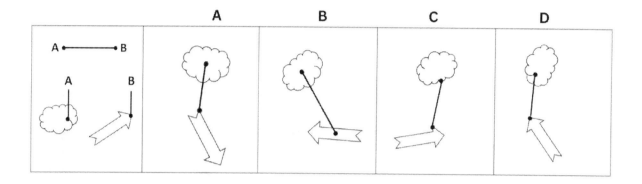

- A
- B
- C
- D

Question 206: Which of these images best shows how to assemble the parts shown in the first picture?

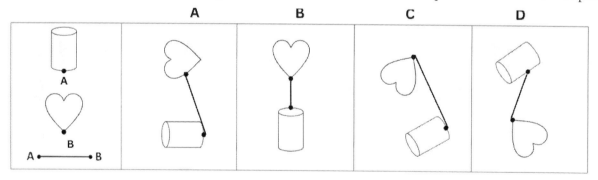

- A
- B
- C
- D

Question 207: For each pair of labeled shapes choose the figure that shows the shapes connected correctly.

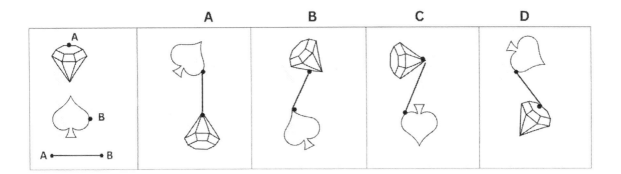

- A
- B
- C
- D

Question 208: For each pair of labeled shapes choose the figure that shows the shapes connected correctly.

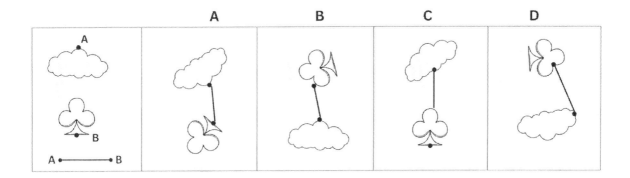

- A
- B
- C
- D

Question 209: Which figure best shows how the objects in the left box will appear if they are fit together?

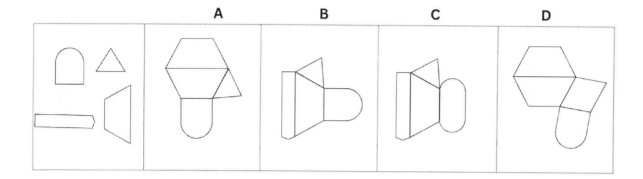

- A
- B
- C
- D

Question 210 Which figure best shows how the objects in the left box will appear if they are fit together?

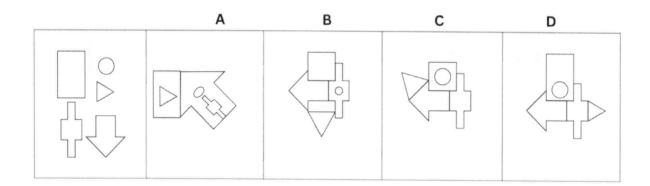

- A
- B
- C
- D

Question 211: Which figure best shows how the objects in the left box will appear if they are fit together?

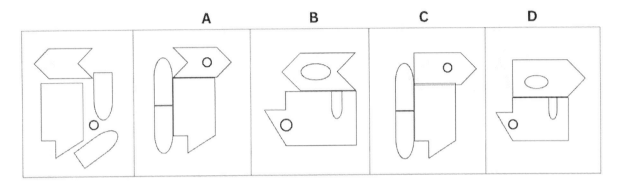

- A
- B
- C
- D

Question 212: Which figure best shows how the objects in the left box will appear if they are fit together?

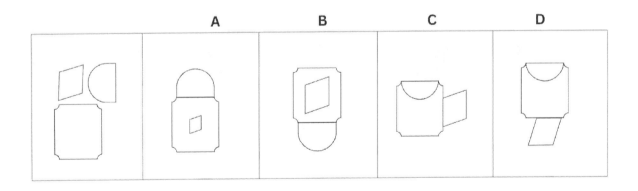

- A
- B
- C
- D

Question 213: Which figure best shows how the objects in the left box will appear if they are fit together?

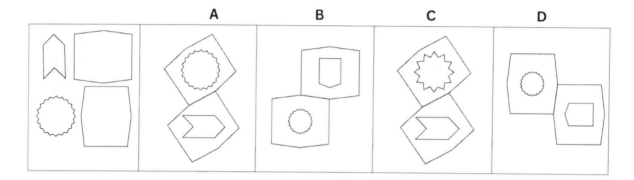

- A
- B
- C
- D

Question 214: Which figure best shows how the objects in the left box will appear if they are fit together?

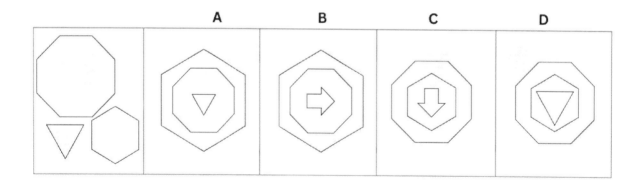

- A
- B
- C
- D

Question 215 Which figure best shows how the objects in the left box will appear if they are fit together?

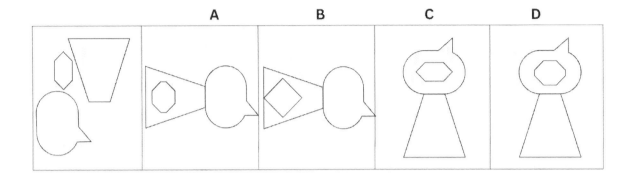

- A
- B
- C
- D

Question 216: Which of the following images best solves the problem in the first picture?

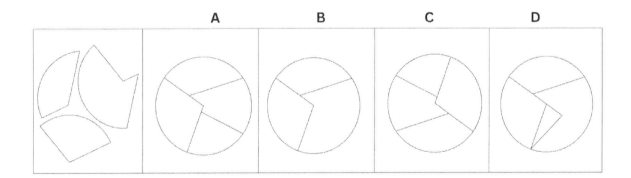

- A
- B
- C
- D

Question 217: Which of the following images best solves the problem in the first picture?

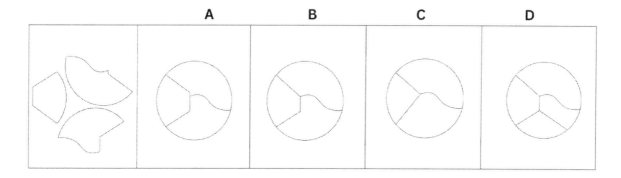

- A
- B
- C
- D

Question 218: Which of the following images best solves the problem in the first picture?

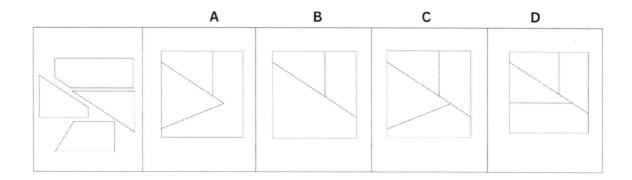

- A
- B
- C
- D

Question 219: Which of the following images best solves the problem in the first picture?

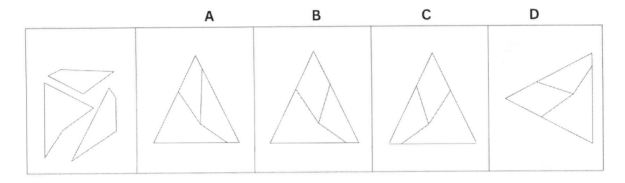

- A
- B
- C
- D

Question 220: Which of the following images best solves the problem in the first picture?

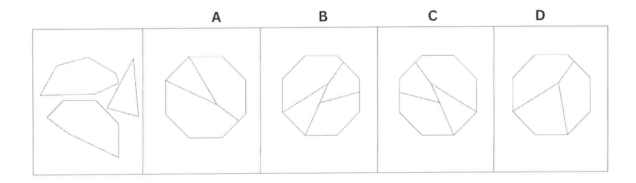

- A
- B
- C
- D

Question 221: Which of the following images best solves the problem in the first picture?

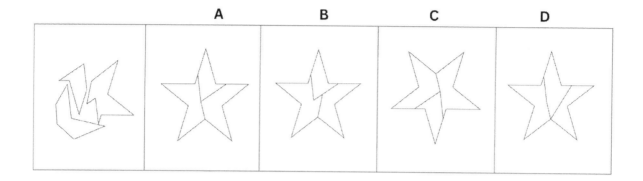

- A
- B
- C
- D

Question 222: Which of the following images best solves the problem in the first picture?

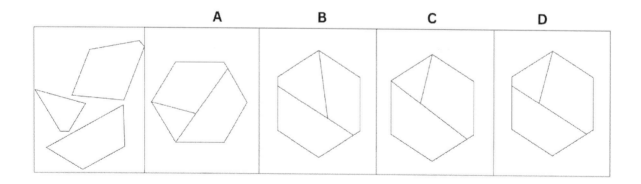

- A
- B
- C
- D

Question 223: Which of the following images best solves the problem in the first picture?

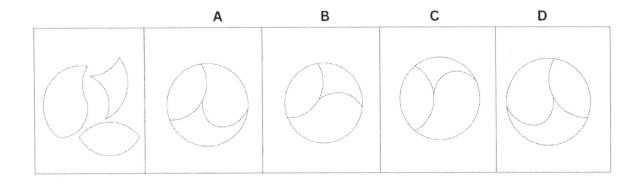

- A
- B
- C
- D

Question 224: Which of the following images best solves the problem in the first picture?

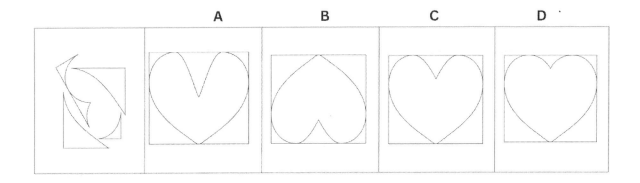

- A
- B
- C
- D

Question 225: Which of the following images best solves the problem in the first picture?

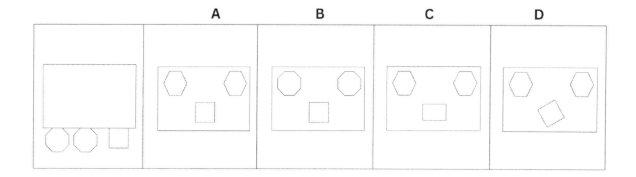

- A
- B
- C
- D

9.2. Answer Key Practice Test

General Science (GS)

1. **Answer:** C. Energy production

   Explanation: The mitochondria are known as the powerhouses of the cell because they produce energy in the form of ATP through cellular respiration.

2. **Answer:** C. Carbon dioxide

   Explanation: Photosynthesis is the process by which plants convert light energy into chemical energy, using carbon dioxide and water to produce glucose and oxygen.

3. **Answer:** A. NaCl

   Explanation: Table salt is composed of sodium (Na) and chlorine (Cl), forming the compound sodium chloride (NaCl).

4. **Answer:** B. Nitrogen

   Explanation: Nitrogen makes up about 78% of the Earth's atmosphere, making it the most abundant gas.

5. **Answer:** A. Nucleus

   Explanation: The nucleus acts as the control center of the cell, containing the genetic material (DNA) that regulates cellular activities.

6. **Answer:** B. Leg

   Explanation: The femur is the thigh bone, which is the longest and strongest bone in the human body, located in the leg.

7. **Answer:** C. Photosynthesis

   Explanation: Photosynthesis is the process by which green plants use sunlight to synthesize foods with the help of chlorophyll.

8. **Answer:** B. Covalent bond

   Explanation: A covalent bond is a chemical bond that involves the sharing of electron pairs between atoms.

9. **Answer:** C. Kidney

   Explanation: The kidneys filter blood to remove waste products and excess substances, which are excreted as urine.

10. **Answer:** B. 7

    Explanation: A pH value of 7 is considered neutral, which is the pH of pure water.

11. **Answer:** B. Mars

    Explanation: Mars is often called the "Red Planet" because of its reddish appearance, which is due to iron oxide (rust) on its surface.

12. **Answer:** C. The sun

    Explanation: The sun is the primary source of energy for the Earth's climate system, driving weather patterns and climate.

13. **Answer:** C. Solar energy

    Explanation: Solar energy is a renewable resource because it is naturally replenished and inexhaustible.

14. **Answer:** C. Igneous

    Explanation: Igneous rocks are formed from the cooling and solidification of magma or lava.

15. **Answer:** D. Root

    Explanation: The roots of a plant are primarily responsible for absorbing water and nutrients from the soil.

16. **Answer:** C. Cell

    Explanation: The cell is the basic unit of life, being the smallest structure capable of performing all the functions necessary for life.

17. **Answer:** C. 100°C

    Explanation: At sea level, water boils at 100°C (212°F).

18. **Answer:** C. Mercury

    Explanation: Mercury is the closest planet to the Sun.

19. **Answer:** B. CO2

    Explanation: The chemical formula for carbon dioxide is CO2.

20. **Answer:** B. Nucleus

    Explanation: The nucleus contains the cell's genetic material (DNA).

21. **Answer:** B. Kidney

    Explanation: The kidneys filter blood to remove waste and excess substances, producing urine.

22. **Answer:** C. Igneous

    Explanation: Igneous rocks form from the cooling and solidification of magma or lava.

23. **Answer:** C. Mitochondria

    Explanation: Mitochondria are known as the powerhouse of the cell because they produce energy.

24. **Answer:** B. Nitrogen

    Explanation: Nitrogen makes up about 78% of the Earth's atmosphere, making it the most abundant gas.

25. **Answer:** C. Carry oxygen

    Explanation: Red blood cells carry oxygen from the lungs to the rest of the body and return carbon dioxide to the lungs for exhalation.

Arithmetic Reasoning (AR)

26. **Answer:** C. 60 mph

    Explanation: Average speed is calculated by dividing the total distance by the total time. 240 miles / 4 hours = 60 mph.

27. **Answer:** C. $4.75

   Explanation: (3 x $0.75) + (2 x $1.25) = $2.25 + $2.50 = $4.75.

28. **Answer:** B. $600

   Explanation: $15 per hour x 40 hours = $600.

29. **Answer:** C. 60 mph

   Explanation: 150 miles / 2.5 hours = 60 mph.

30. **Answer:** B. 1/3 cup

   Explanation: (2/3 cup) x (1/2) = 2/6 cup = 1/3 cup.

31. **Answer:** B. 8

   Explanation: 4 bags x 6 apples = 24 apples; 24 apples / 3 friends = 8 apples per friend.

32. **Answer:** C. $100

   Explanation: Let the original price be x. 20% discount means the sale price is 80% of the original price. 0.8x = 80; x = 80 / 0.8 = $100.

33. **Answer:** C. $5

   Explanation: 15 oranges / 3 oranges per dollar = 5 dollars.

34. **Answer:** A. $18.75

   Explanation: $50 - $18.75 - $12.50 = $18.75.

35. **Answer:** B. $43.20

   Explanation: Total cost without discount = 4 x $12 = $48. 10% discount = 0.1 x $48 = $4.80. Total cost with discount = $48 - $4.80 = $43.20.

36. **Answer:** B. 2:3

   Explanation: Ratio of pigs to cows = 10 pigs / 15 cows = 2/3 = 2:3.

37. **Answer:** B. 4 hours

   Explanation: If the number of workers doubles, the time required is halved. 8 hours / 2 = 4 hours.

38. **Answer:** B. 86.25

   Explanation: (85 + 90 + 78 + 92) / 4 = 345 / 4 = 86.25.

39. **Answer:** C. 20 minutes

   Explanation: 500 gallons / 25 gallons per minute = 20 minutes.

40. **Answer:** C. $920

   Explanation: 15% of $800 = 0.15 x $800 = $120. New price = $800 + $120 = $920.

41. **Answer:** C. 25 mpg

   Explanation: 300 miles / 12 gallons = 25 miles per gallon.

42. Answer: B. 18

Explanation: Ratio of boys to girls = 3:4. Let the number of boys be 3x and girls be 4x. 4x = 24; x = 6. Number of boys = 3x = 3 x 6 = 18.

43. Answer: C. $400

Explanation: Let the original price be x. 25% discount means the sale price is 75% of the original price. 0.75x = 300; x = 300 / 0.75 = $400.

44. Answer: D. 32 meters

Explanation: Perimeter of a rectangle = 2(length + width). 2(10 + 6) = 2 x 16 = 32 meters.

45. Answer: C. 3/10

Explanation: Probability = (Number of desired outcomes) / (Total number of outcomes). Probability of drawing a red ball = 3 / (3 + 2 + 5) = 3/10.

46. Answer: C. $26

Explanation: Total cost = 3 x $8 + $2 = $24 + $2 = $26.

47. Answer: C. $180.80

Explanation: Total cost without discount = $150 + $30 + $20 = $200. 10% discount = 0.1 x $200 = $20. Total cost with discount = $200 - $20 = $180.80.

48. Answer: D. 150 square meters

Explanation: Area = length x width = 15 meters x 10 meters = 150 square meters.

49. Answer: B. $25

Explanation: Interest = Principal x Rate x Time. Interest = $500 x 0.05 x 1 = $25.

50. Answer: C. 300

Explanation: Number of girls = 60% of 500 = 0.6 x 500 = 300.

51. Answer: C. $55

Explanation: Cost = (daily rate x number of days) + (cost per mile x number of miles). Cost = (20 x 3) + (0.10 x 150) = $60 + $15 = $75.

52. Answer: C. $20

Explanation: 20% of $25 = 0.20 x $25 = $5. Sale price = $25 - $5 = $20.

53. Answer: D. 15 gallons

Explanation: 450 miles / 30 miles per gallon = 15 gallons.

54. Answer: B. $450

Explanation: 25% of $600 = 0.25 x $600 = $150. Sale price = $600 - $150 = $450.

55. Answer: C. 3/8 cup

Explanation: (3/4 cup) x (1/2) = 3/8 cup.

Word Knowledge (WK)

56. Answer: B. Friendly

Explanation: "Gregarious" means sociable or enjoying the company of others, which is most closely related to "friendly."

57. Answer: C. Careful

Explanation: "Prudent" means acting with or showing care and thought for the future, which is best described by "careful."

58. Answer: C. Outdated

Explanation: "Obsolete" means no longer in use or out of date, which is synonymous with "outdated."

59. Answer: B. Talkative

Explanation: "Verbose" means using more words than needed, which is closely related to "talkative."

60. Answer: B. Kind

Explanation: "Benevolent" means well-meaning and kindly, which is synonymous with "kind."

61. Answer: C. Compel

Explanation: "Coerce" means to force someone to do something, which is closely related to "compel."

62. Answer: B. Hardworking

Explanation: "Diligent" means showing care and conscientiousness in one's work or duties, which is best described by "hardworking."

63. Answer: C. Lessen

Explanation: "Mitigate" means to make less severe or serious, which is synonymous with "lessen."

64. Answer: B. Honest

Explanation: "Candid" means truthful and straightforward, which is best described by "honest."

65. Answer: B. Imitate

Explanation: "Emulate" means to match or surpass, typically by imitation, which is closely related to "imitate."

66. Answer: B. Clear

Explanation: "Lucid" means expressed clearly or easy to understand, which is synonymous with "clear."

67. Answer: B. Hostility

Explanation: "Animosity" means strong hostility, which is best described by "hostility."

68. Answer: B. Difficult

Explanation: "Arduous" means involving or requiring strenuous effort, which is synonymous with "difficult."

69. Answer: B. Showy

Explanation: "Ostentatious" means characterized by vulgar or pretentious display, which is best described by "showy."

70. Answer: B. Soothe

Explanation: "Placate" means to make someone less angry or hostile, which is closely related to "soothe."

71. Answer: B. Fruitful

Explanation: "Prolific" means producing much fruit or foliage or many offspring, which is synonymous with "fruitful."

72. Answer: B. Justify

Explanation: "Vindicate" means to clear someone of blame or suspicion, which is closely related to "justify."

73. Answer: C. Unyielding

Explanation: "Adamant" means refusing to be persuaded or to change one's mind, which is best described by "unyielding."

74. Answer: B. Wicked

Explanation: "Nefarious" means wicked or criminal, which is synonymous with "wicked."

75. Answer: C. Brief

Explanation: "Ephemeral" means lasting for a very short time, which is best described by "brief."

76. Answer: C. Thrifty

Explanation: "Frugal" means sparing or economical with regard to money or food, which is synonymous with "thrifty."

77. Answer: B. Passionate

Explanation: "Ardent" means enthusiastic or passionate, which is best described by "passionate."

78. Answer: B. Flexible

Explanation: "Malleable" means capable of being shaped or bent, which is closely related to "flexible."

79. Answer: B. Generous

Explanation: "Altruistic" means showing a disinterested and selfless concern for the well-being of others, which is synonymous with "generous."

80. Answer: B. Abundant

Explanation: "Copious" means large in quantity or number, which is best described by "abundant."

81. Answer: C. Evasive

Explanation: "Elusive" means difficult to find, catch, or achieve, which is synonymous with "evasive."

82. Answer: C. Unfeeling

Explanation: "Callous" means showing or having an insensitive and cruel disregard for others, which is best described by "unfeeling."

83. Answer: B. Persistent

Explanation: "Tenacious" means tending to keep a firm hold of something, which is synonymous with "persistent."

84. Answer: A. Sociable

Explanation: "Gregarious" means fond of company or sociable, which is closely related to "sociable."

85. Answer: B. Careless

Explanation: "Perfunctory" means carried out with a minimum of effort or reflection, which is best described by "careless."

86. Answer: B. Omnipresent

Explanation: "Ubiquitous" means present, appearing, or found everywhere, which is synonymous with "omnipresent."

87. Answer: B. Quiet

Explanation: "Laconic" means using very few words, which is closely related to "quiet."

88. Answer: B. Inborn

Explanation: "Innate" means inborn or natural, which is best described by "inborn."

89. Answer: B. Enthusiastic

Explanation: "Zealous" means having or showing zeal, which is synonymous with "enthusiastic."

90. Answer: B. Concise

Explanation: "Succinct" means briefly and clearly expressed, which is best described by "concise."

Paragraph Comprehension (PC)

91. Answer: D. Technology has reduced the need for some manual labor jobs.

Explanation: The passage states that automation and artificial intelligence have increased efficiency and reduced the need for manual labor, implying that some manual jobs have been affected.

92. Answer: A. Calm

Explanation: The passage describes the lake as peaceful and a contrast to the bustling city, indicating that "serene" means calm.

93. Answer: B. To protect against invasions

Explanation: The passage explicitly states that the Great Wall of China was built to protect against invasions.

94. Answer: B. To reduce their carbon footprint

Explanation: The passage mentions that people are turning to renewable energy sources to reduce their carbon footprint and combat climate change.

95. Answer: C. It absorbs large amounts of carbon dioxide

Explanation: The passage explains that the Amazon Rainforest is called the "lungs of the Earth" because it plays a critical role in absorbing carbon dioxide.

96. Answer: D. Increasing appetite

Explanation: The passage lists improving cardiovascular health, strengthening muscles, and enhancing mental well-being as benefits of regular exercise but does not mention increasing appetite.

97. Answer: C. Allowing instant global connections

Explanation: The passage states that the internet allows people to connect instantly across the globe, indicating its impact on global communication.

98. Answer: B. Cultural and intellectual advancements

Explanation: The passage states that the Renaissance led to significant cultural and intellectual advancements.

99. Answer: C. To carry out photosynthesis

Explanation: The passage explains that the primary function of leaves is to perform photosynthesis.

100. **Answer:** C. Staying on designated paths

    Explanation: The passage mentions that visitors must stay on designated paths to help preserve the historical site.

101. **Answer:** B. To improve critical thinking skills

    Explanation: The passage states that the primary goal of the educational program is to enhance students' critical thinking skills.

102. **Answer:** C. Focusing on innovation and customer satisfaction

    Explanation: The passage indicates that the company increased its revenue by focusing on innovation and customer satisfaction.

103. **Answer:** C. Sustainability

    Explanation: The passage mentions that the architect designed the building with sustainability in mind.

104. **Answer:** B. To reduce traffic congestion

    Explanation: The passage states that the policy aims to reduce traffic congestion.

105. **Answer:** B. Understanding climate change

    Explanation: The passage explains that the scientist's research provided new insights into the causes of climate change.

Mathematics Knowledge (MK)

106. **Answer:** C. 40 square meters

    Explanation: Area = length x width = 8 meters x 5 meters = 40 square meters.

107. **Answer:** D. 16

    Explanation: $3x + 2y = 3(4) + 2(2) = 12 + 4 = 16$

108. **Answer:** C. 5

    Explanation: $2x - 3 = 7 \Rightarrow 2x = 10 \Rightarrow x = 5$

109. **Answer:** C. 27 cubic cm

    Explanation: Volume = side length^3 = 33 = $3 \times 3 \times 3 = 27$ *cubic cm.*

110. **Answer:** B. 12x - 20

    Explanation: $4(3x - 5) = 12x - 204(3x - 5) = 12x - 204(3x - 5) = 12x - 20$

111. **Answer:** B. 18

    Explanation: $[\frac{a^2}{b} = \frac{6^2}{2} = \frac{36}{2} = 18]$

112. **Answer: C. 5**

Explanation: $3y + 4 = 19 \Rightarrow 3y = 15 \Rightarrow y = 5$

113. **Answer:** A. 10 cm

Explanation: By the Pythagorean theorem, hypotenuse = [hypotenuse = $\sqrt{6^2 + 8^2}$ = $\sqrt{36 + 64} = \sqrt{100} = 10$ cm]

114. **Answer:** C. 30

Explanation: $15\%15\backslash\%15\%$ of $200 = 0.15 \times 200 = 300.15 \times 200 = 300.15 \times 200 = 30.$

115. **Answer:** D. 26

Explanation: $If\ (\ x\ =\ -3\ ): x^2 - 4x + 5 = (-3)^2 - 4(-3) + 5 = 9 + 12 + 5 = 26$

116. **Answer:** C. 3

Explanation: The slope m is calculated as: $m = \frac{11-3}{5-2} = \frac{8}{3}$. Therefore, the slope is 3.

117. **Answer:** Answer: A. x−4

Explanation:$[\frac{2x^2-8x}{2x} = \frac{2x(x-4)}{2x} = x - 4$

118. **Answer:** B. 0.035

Explanation: To convert 3.5% to a decimal, divide by 100:$3.5\backslash\% = \frac{3.5}{100} = 0.035$

119. **Answer:** D.

Explanation: $5x - 2 = 3x + 8 \Rightarrow 2x - 2 = 8 \Rightarrow 2x = 10 \Rightarrow x = 5$

120. **Answer: B. 28 cm**

Explanation: Perimeter = 7 cm + 9 cm + 12 cm = 28 cm.

121. **Answer:** B. $12x^3y^3$

Explanation: $(3x^2y)(4xy^2) = 12x^3y^3$

122. **Answer:** C. 4 cm

Explanation: $16\pi = \pi r^2 \Rightarrow 16 = r^2 \Rightarrow r = 4$ cm

123. **Answer: C.**

Explanation: $4z - 7 = 13 \Rightarrow 4z = 20 \Rightarrow z = 5$

124. **Answer:** D. 120

Explanation: $5! = 5 \times 4 \times 3 \times 2 \times 1 = 120$

125. **Answer:** C. 11

Explanation: $x + 2 = 7 \Rightarrow x = 5$

$$2x + 1 = 2(5) + 1 = 11$$

126. **Answer:** C. $(5, 7)$

   Explanation: *The midpoint formula is:* $\left[\left(\frac{x_1+x_2}{2}, \frac{y_1+y_2}{2}\right)\right]$

   $$Midpoint\ formula: \left(\frac{2+8}{2}, \frac{3+11}{2}\right) = (5,7)\ Therefore, the\ midpoint\ is (5,7)$$

127. **Answer:** B. 3

   Explanation: $2y + 3 = 9 \Rightarrow 2y = 6 \Rightarrow y = 3$

128. **Answer:** C. 6 cm

   Explanation: Perimeter of a square $= 4\ x\ side\ length.$

   $24 = 4 \times$ side length

   $$side\ length = \frac{24}{4} = 6\ cm$$

129. **Answer:** B. 0.008

   Explanation: $8 \times 10^{-3} = 0.008$

130. **Answer:** D. 25

   Explanation: $x^2 + y^2 = 3^2 + 4^2 = 9 + 16 = 25$

Electronics Information (EI) 20

131. **Answer:** C. Ampere

   Explanation: The ampere (A) is the unit of electric current in the International System of Units (SI).

132. **Answer:** B. Capacitor

   Explanation: A capacitor stores electrical energy in an electric field between its plates.

133. **Answer:** B. Alternating current (AC)

   Explanation: Household electrical outlets in the United States supply alternating current(AC).

134. **Answer:** C. To allow current to flow in only one direction

   Explanation: A diode allows current to flow in only one direction and blocks it in the opposite direction.

135. **Answer:** D. Transformer

   Explanation: A transformer is used to step up or step down AC voltage levels.

136.   Answer: C. To protect the circuit by breaking the connection in case of an overload

Explanation: A fuse protects the circuit by breaking the connection when the current exceeds a certain level, preventing damage to the circuit.

137.   Answer: A. Light Emitting Diode

Explanation: LED stands for Light Emitting Diode, a semiconductor device that emits light when an electric current passes through it.

138.   Answer: B. 2 amperes

Explanation: Using Ohm's Law $(V = IR)$, the current (I) is calculated as follows:

$I = \frac{V}{R} = \frac{12 \text{ volts}}{6 \text{ ohms}} = 2$ amperes. Thus, the current in the circuit is 2 amperes.

139.   Answer: D. Transistor

Explanation: A transistor is a semiconductor device used to amplify or switch electronic signals and electrical power.

140.   Answer: B. To adjust voltage

Explanation: A potentiometer is a variable resistor used to adjust voltage in a circuit.

141.   Answer: B. To store energy in a magnetic field

Explanation: An inductor stores energy in a magnetic field when electric current passes through it.

142.   Answer: C. Ohmmeter

Explanation: An ohmmeter is used to measure electrical resistance.

143.   Answer: C. Faster switching speed

Explanation: Transistors have faster switching speeds and are smaller and more efficient than vacuum tubes.

144.   Answer: C. To limit current

Explanation: A resistor limits the amount of current flowing through an electronic circuit.

145.   Answer: A. Zigzag line

Explanation: A zigzag line represents a resistor in a circuit diagram.

146.   Answer: B. 1.5 volts

Explanation: A standard AA battery typically has a voltage of 1.5 volts.

147.   Answer: C. To open or close the circuit

Explanation: A switch is used to open or close an electrical circuit, controlling the flow of current.

148.   Answer: B. A point of reference for voltage levels

Explanation: In electronics, "ground" refers to a common return path for electric current, serving as a reference point for voltage levels.

149. **Answer:** B. To convert AC to DC

Explanation: A rectifier converts alternating current (AC) to direct current (DC).

150. **Answer:** C. Fuse

Explanation: A fuse protects electronic circuits by breaking the connection when excessive current flows through it.

Auto and Shop Information (AS)

151. **Answer:** C. Hammer

Explanation: A hammer is commonly used to drive nails into wood.

152. **Answer:** A. Radiator

Explanation: The radiator cools the engine by circulating coolant through the engine and releasing the heat through the radiator fins.

153. **Answer:** B. Charges the battery and powers the electrical system when the engine is running

Explanation: The alternator charges the vehicle's battery and powers the electrical system while the engine is running.

154. **Answer:** D. Dial bore gauge

Explanation: A dial bore gauge is used to measure the internal diameter of a cylinder with high accuracy.

155. **Answer:** A. To measure the force applied to a fastener

Explanation: A torque wrench is used to apply a specific amount of force to a fastener, ensuring it is tightened correctly.

156. **Answer:** A. Electronic Fuel Injection

Explanation: EFI stands for Electronic Fuel Injection, a system that delivers fuel to the engine electronically.

157. **Answer:** C. Jigsaw

Explanation: A jigsaw is designed for cutting curves and intricate shapes in wood.

158. **Answer:** B. Exhaust system

Explanation: The catalytic converter is part of the exhaust system and reduces harmful emissions from the engine.

159. **Answer:** B. To lubricate engine parts

Explanation: Engine oil lubricates moving parts within the engine to reduce friction and wear.

160. **Answer:** B. Feeler gauge

Explanation: A feeler gauge is used to measure the gap between the electrodes of a spark plug.

161. **Answer:** C. Ceramic

Explanation: Ceramic is a common material used for brake pads due to its durability and heat resistance.

162. **Answer:** A. Crankshaft

Explanation: The crankshaft converts the linear motion of the pistons into rotational motion to power the vehicle.

163. **Answer:** A. Wire stripper

Explanation: A wire stripper is used to remove the insulation from electrical wires without damaging the wire itself.

164. **Answer:** B. To reduce exhaust noise

Explanation: The muffler reduces the noise produced by the exhaust gases as they exit the vehicle.

165. **Answer:** C. Fusion joint

Explanation: Welding creates a fusion joint by melting and fusing materials together.

166. **Answer:** B. Anvil

Explanation: An anvil is used as a sturdy surface to shape metal by hammering.

167. **Answer:** C. To regulate the engine temperature

Explanation: Coolant helps regulate the engine temperature by absorbing heat and dissipating it through the radiator.

168. **Answer:** A. Tap

Explanation: A tap is used to create internal threads in a hole.

169. **Answer:** B. Shock absorber

Explanation: The shock absorber absorbs and dampens shocks from the road to provide a smooth ride.

170. **Answer:** C. Triangular file

Explanation: A triangular file is commonly used to sharpen saw blades.

171. **Answer:** B. To change gears

Explanation: The clutch allows the driver to change gears by temporarily disconnecting the engine from the transmission.

172. **Answer:** C. Adjustable wrench

Explanation: An adjustable wrench can be adjusted to fit hex and square bolts of various sizes.

173.   **Answer:** C. To smooth and finish wood surfaces

Explanation: Sandpaper is used to smooth and finish wood surfaces by abrasion.

174.   **Answer:** B. Camshaft

Explanation: The camshaft controls the opening and closing of the engine's valves.

175.   **Answer:** B. To smooth and flatten wood surfaces

Explanation: A planer is used to smooth and flatten wood surfaces by shaving off thin layers of wood.

Mechanical Comprehension (MC)

176.   **Answer:** B. Pulley

Explanation: A pulley consists of a wheel with a rope or cable that can be used to lift heavy objects.

177.   **Answer:** D. 4

Explanation: The mechanical advantage of a lever is calculated by dividing the length of the effort arm by the length of the resistance arm. $\text{MA} = \frac{L_e}{L_r} = \frac{4\,\text{m}}{1\,\text{m}} = 4$

178.   **Answer:** B. To lift heavy objects

Explanation: A hydraulic jack uses fluid pressure to lift heavy objects.

179.   **Answer:** C. Archimedes' principle

Explanation: Archimedes' principle states that a body submerged in a fluid is buoyed up by a force equal to the weight of the displaced fluid, which explains why ships float.

180.   **Answer:** B. Bevel gear

Explanation: Bevel gears are used to change the direction of rotational motion by 90 degrees.

181.   **Answer:** A. To store rotational energy

Explanation: A flywheel stores rotational energy to smooth out the power delivery of the engine.

182.   **Answer:** A. To reduce friction

Explanation: Ball bearings reduce friction between moving parts by providing smooth surfaces that roll rather than slide.

183.   **Answer:** C. 4

Explanation: Mechanical advantage is $\text{MA} = \frac{F_{\text{out}}}{F_{\text{in}}} = \frac{200\,\text{N}}{50\,\text{N}} = 4$

184.   **Answer:** C. Inclined plane

Explanation: A ramp is an inclined plane, which allows heavy objects to be moved upwards with less effort.

185. **Answer:** B. To stop the vehicle by creating friction

Explanation: The brake drum creates friction against the brake shoes, helping to stop the vehicle.

186. **Answer:** C. To transfer force

Explanation: In a hydraulic system, the fluid transfers force from one point to another.

187. **Answer:** C. Newton's third law

Explanation: Newton's third law states that for every action, there is an equal and opposite reaction.

188. **Answer:** B. Rotational motion to linear motion

Explanation: A camshaft converts rotational motion into linear motion to operate the engine's valves.

189. **Answer:** D. 4

Explanation: The mechanical advantage of a pulley system is equal to the number of supporting ropes.

190. **Answer:** C. Watt

Explanation: The watt is the SI unit of power, defined as one joule per second.

191. **Answer:** C. To change the speed and torque

Explanation: A gear ratio changes the speed and torque in a mechanical system.

192. **Answer:** A. The fulcrum is located between the effort and the load

Explanation: In a first-class lever, the fulcrum is positioned between the effort and the load.

193. **Answer:** D. Wheel and axle

Explanation: A bicycle wheel and axle is a simple machine that consists of a large wheel attached to a smaller axle.

194. **Answer:** C. To protect the circuit by breaking the connection if the current is too high

Explanation: A fuse protects an electrical circuit by breaking the connection if the current exceeds a certain level, preventing damage to the circuit.

195. **Answer:** B. Piston

Explanation: The piston converts the chemical energy of the fuel into mechanical energy by moving up and down in the cylinder.

196. **Answer:** B. To store and release energy

Explanation: A spring stores mechanical energy when compressed or stretched and releases it when returned to its original shape.

197. **Answer:** C. Inclined plane

Explanation: A screw is considered an inclined plane wrapped around a cylinder.

198.   **Answer:** C. Increased mechanical advantage

Explanation: A compound pulley system increases the mechanical advantage, making it easier to lift heavy objects.

199.   **Answer:** D. Bernoulli's principle

Explanation: Bernoulli's principle states that the pressure in a fluid decreases as the fluid's velocity increases.

200.   **Answer:** B. Camshaft

Explanation: A camshaft converts rotational motion into reciprocating motion to operate the engine's valves.

Assembling Objects (AO)

201.   **Answer:** C

202.   **Answer** A

203.   **Answer:** B

204.   **Answer:** A

205.   **Answer:** D

206.   **Answer:** C

207.   **Answer** D

208.   **Answer:** A

209.   **Answer:** B

210.   **Answer:** D

211.   **Answer:** A

212.   **Answer:** B

213.   **Answer:** A

214.   **Answer:** D

215.   **Answer:** C

216.   **Answer:** B

217.   **Answer:** A

218.   **Answer:** D

219.   **Answer:** A

220.   **Answer:** A

221.   **Answer:** B

222.   **Answer:** D

223.   **Answer:** B

224.   **Answer:** D

225.   **Answer:** B

9.5 Identifying Areas for Improvement

After reviewing both practice tests, it's important to analyze your performance and identify areas where you need further study and practice. Here are some steps to help you focus your efforts:

Analyze Your Results:

- **Identify Weak Areas**: Look at the sections where you scored the lowest and identify the specific topics or types of questions that were challenging for you.

- **Note Patterns**: Observe any patterns in your mistakes, such as specific concepts you consistently got wrong or question types that gave you trouble.

Focus on Weak Areas:

- **Devote Study Time**: Spend additional study time on the topics and question types you found most difficult. Use the explanations provided in the answer keys to guide your review.

- **Practice More**: Work on more questions in these areas to build your confidence and improve your accuracy.

Seek Additional Resources:

- **Study Guides and Online Resources**: Utilize additional study guides, online resources, and practice questions to reinforce your understanding of challenging topics.

- **Study Groups and Tutors**: Consider joining a study group or seeking help from a tutor if you need more personalized assistance.

Track Your Progress:

- **Monitor Scores**: Keep track of your scores and progress over time. Tracking your improvements can boost your confidence and help you stay motivated.

- **Set Goals**: Establish specific goals for each study session and work towards achieving them.

Maintain a Positive Mindset:

- **Stay Positive**: Remember that improvement takes time and effort. Stay positive and keep working towards your goal.
- **Celebrate Successes**: Celebrate your achievements and progress, no matter how small, to stay motivated and focused.

By taking these steps to identify and address your areas for improvement, you can enhance your preparation for the ASVAB and increase your chances of achieving a high score. Consistent practice, thorough review, and a positive attitude will help you succeed on test day.

Take your preparation to the next level with our exclusive bonus content!

Download the **2500+ Q&A Explained** for comprehensive practice and detailed explanations. This invaluable resource will help you understand the reasoning behind each answer, ensuring you grasp the concepts and are fully prepared for every section of the ASVAB.

Don't miss out on this essential tool—scan the QR code below to download now and maximize your study efforts!

GET YOUR EXTRA CONTENTS NOW!

TO DOWNLOAD YOUR BONUS SCAN THE CODE BELOW

This bonus is 100% FREE, no strings attached

Or visit https://rebrand.ly/615c65

Chapter 10: Mapping Your Military Career

10.1. Understanding Military Job Placements

Each branch of the military offers a variety of roles, known as Military Occupational Specialties (MOS) in the Army and Marine Corps, Ratings in the Navy, and Air Force Specialty Codes (AFSC) in the Air Force. These roles require different skills and aptitudes, which are assessed through the ASVAB.

Key Points

- **Job Classifications**: Each job within the military has specific requirements and qualifications. Your ASVAB scores will determine which jobs you are eligible for.

- **Importance of ASVAB Scores**: Higher ASVAB scores can qualify you for more specialized and desirable roles. It's important to aim for the best possible scores to expand your career options.

- **Training and Education**: Depending on your MOS, Rating, or AFSC, you will receive specialized training to prepare you for your duties. This training is crucial for your success in your chosen career path.

10.2 Matching ASVAB Scores with Military Jobs

Each branch of the military uses different combinations of ASVAB subtest scores to create composite scores that qualify you for various jobs.

Army:

- **Clerical (CL)**: VE + AR + MK

- **Combat (CO)**: AR + CS + MK + VE

- **Electronics (EL)**: GS + AR + MK + EI

- **General Technical (GT)**: VE + AR

- **Mechanical Maintenance (MM)**: NO + AS + MC + EI

- **Skilled Technical (ST)**: GS + VE + MK + MC

Navy:

- **Engineering and Physical Science (EP)**: AR + MK + EI + GS

- **General Technical (GT)**: VE + MK + MC + AR

- **Mechanical Maintenance (MM)**: AR + VE + AS + MC

- **Nuclear Field (NF)**: AR + MK + EI + GS

Air Force:

- **Administrative (A)**: VE + MK

- **Electronics (E)**: AR + MK + EI + GS

- **General (G)**: VE + AR

- **Mechanical (M)**: ME + AS + MC + AR

Marine Corps:

- **General Technical (GT)**: VE + AR

- **Electronics Repair (EL)**: GS + AR + MK + EI

- **Mechanical Maintenance (MM)**: NO + AS + MC + EI

- **Clerical (CL)**: VE + AR + MK

- **Skilled Technical (ST)**: GS + VE + MK + MC

10.3 Exploring Different Military Branches

Each branch of the military offers unique career opportunities and experiences. Understanding the differences between the branches can help you make an informed decision about where to enlist.

Army:

- The largest branch of the military, offering a wide range of roles in combat, engineering, intelligence, logistics, and medical fields.

- Known for its strong emphasis on leadership development and career progression.

Navy:

- Focuses on naval and maritime operations, offering careers in aviation, engineering, intelligence, and medical fields.

- Provides opportunities for travel and deployment around the world.

Air Force:

- Specializes in air and space operations, with careers in aviation, cyber operations, intelligence, and engineering.
- Emphasizes advanced technology and innovation.

Marine Corps:

- Known for its rapid-response capabilities and focus on amphibious and expeditionary warfare.
- Offers roles in combat, aviation, logistics, and intelligence.

Coast Guard:

- Focuses on maritime safety, security, and environmental protection.
- Offers careers in law enforcement, search and rescue, and environmental response.

10.4 Planning Your Career Path

Planning your military career involves setting goals, understanding the progression within your chosen field, and taking advantage of opportunities for advancement and education.

Setting Goals:

- **Short-Term Goals**: Focus on immediate objectives, such as achieving high ASVAB scores, completing basic training, and mastering your initial MOS or Rating.
- **Long-Term Goals**: Consider your long-term career aspirations, such as advancing to higher ranks, transitioning to specialized roles, or pursuing further education and training.

Career Progression:

- **Advancement Opportunities**: Each branch offers opportunities for promotion and advancement based on performance, experience, and education.
- **Specialized Training**: Take advantage of specialized training programs to enhance your skills and qualifications for advanced roles.

Education and Benefits:

- **Tuition Assistance**: Many branches offer tuition assistance programs to help you pursue higher education while serving.
- **GI Bill**: The GI Bill provides financial support for education and training after you leave the military.
- **Certifications**: Earn professional certifications related to your field, which can enhance your career prospects both within and outside the military.

10.5 Interview with a Career Counselor

Speaking with a career counselor can provide valuable insights and guidance as you plan your military career. Career counselors can help you understand your options, set realistic goals, and make informed decisions about your future.

Key Questions to Ask:

- What career options are available based on my ASVAB scores?
- How can I improve my chances of qualifying for my desired MOS or Rating?
- What are the promotion and advancement opportunities in my chosen field?
- What educational benefits and programs are available to me?
- How can I prepare for specialized training and advanced roles?

Preparing for the Interview:

- **Research Your Options**: Before meeting with a career counselor, research the different career paths and opportunities available in your chosen branch.
- **Know Your Scores**: Have a clear understanding of your ASVAB scores and how they relate to different military jobs.
- **Set Clear Goals**: Think about your short-term and long-term career goals and be prepared to discuss them with the counselor.

Follow-Up:

- **Take Notes**: During the interview, take notes on the advice and information provided by the career counselor.
- **Create an Action Plan**: Based on the counselor's guidance, create an action plan to achieve your career goals.
- **Seek Further Guidance**: Don't hesitate to schedule follow-up meetings with your career counselor as you progress in your military career.

By understanding military job placements, matching your ASVAB scores with suitable roles, exploring different branches, planning your career path, and seeking guidance from a career counselor, you can successfully navigate your military career and achieve your professional goals.

Conclusion

As you prepare to take the ASVAB and embark on your military career, remember that this journey is not just about passing a test. It's about setting the foundation for a future filled with opportunities and growth. The knowledge and skills you've gained through your preparation will serve you well, not only on the ASVAB but throughout your military service and beyond.

Every step you've taken to understand the test format, improve your verbal and mathematical skills, enhance your spatial reasoning, and build your confidence has brought you closer to achieving your goals. Your dedication and hard work are the keys to unlocking your potential and succeeding in the military.

Transitioning from preparation to success involves maintaining the habits and strategies you've developed. Here are some final tips to help you carry your preparation into the test and beyond:

- **Consistent Practice:** Continue practicing regularly up until the day of the test. Consistent practice helps reinforce your knowledge and keeps your skills sharp.
- **Utilize Test-Taking Strategies:** Apply the test-taking strategies you've learned, such as time management, answer elimination, and staying calm and focused. These strategies will help you navigate the test effectively.
- **Review and Reflect:** After the test, take time to review and reflect on your performance. Identify areas where you excelled and areas where you can improve. Use this insight to guide your future study and career efforts.
- **Stay Positive:** Maintain a positive attitude throughout the process. Confidence and a positive mindset can significantly impact your performance and overall experience.
- The journey to a successful military career will present both challenges and achievements. Embracing these experiences is essential for personal and professional growth.

Facing Challenges:
- o **Adaptability:** Be prepared to adapt to new situations and challenges. The military environment is dynamic, and the ability to adapt is crucial.
- o **Resilience:** Develop resilience to overcome setbacks and continue striving towards your goals. Challenges are opportunities for growth and learning.

ASVAB Study Guide

Celebrating Achievements:

- o **Recognize Milestones:** Celebrate your achievements, both big and small. Recognizing your progress keeps you motivated and focused.
- o **Share Successes:** Share your successes with family, friends, and mentors. Their support and encouragement can boost your morale and keep you grounded.

As you stand on the threshold of your military career, remember that you have the skills, knowledge, and determination to succeed. The ASVAB is just the beginning of an exciting and rewarding journey. Remember to:

Believe in Yourself: Have confidence in your abilities and trust in the preparation you've done. You are capable of achieving great things.

Stay Focused: Keep your goals in sight and stay focused on the path ahead. Your dedication and hard work will pay off.

Seek Support: Don't hesitate to seek support from mentors, peers, and family. Their guidance and encouragement can help you navigate challenges and celebrate successes.

Keep Learning: The military is a place of continuous learning and growth. Embrace every opportunity to learn new skills and gain new experiences.

Make a Difference: Remember that your service is making a difference. Whether you're protecting your country, helping others, or advancing your career, your contributions are valuable and meaningful.

Thank you for choosing this guide to prepare for the ASVAB. Your decision to use this resource demonstrates your dedication to securing a bright future, and we are confident you have made a wise choice. Stay positive, stay focused, and seize the opportunities that await you. The future is bright, and you hold the power to shape it. Good luck, and thank you for your service.

Appendix

Glossary of Key Terms

A

Adaptive Test: A type of test where the difficulty of questions adjusts based on the test-taker's responses.

AFQT (Armed Forces Qualification Test): A score derived from four subtests of the ASVAB (Arithmetic Reasoning, Mathematics Knowledge, Paragraph Comprehension, and Word Knowledge) used to determine eligibility for enlistment in the U.S. Armed Forces.

Algorithm: A step-by-step procedure for solving a problem or accomplishing some end.

Algebra: A branch of mathematics dealing with symbols and the rules for manipulating those symbols, used to express and solve equations.

Altitude: The height of an object or point in relation to sea level or ground level.

Ampere (A): The unit of electric current in the International System of Units (SI).

Amplitude: In physics, the maximum extent of a vibration or oscillation, measured from the position of equilibrium.

Analog: A type of signal or data that varies continuously over time and can take on a range of values.

Angle: A figure formed by two rays, called the sides of the angle, sharing a common endpoint, called the vertex of the angle.

Anode: The positively charged electrode by which the electrons leave a device.

Antibody: A blood protein produced in response to and counteracting a specific antigen. Antibodies are part of the immune system and help to identify and neutralize foreign objects like bacteria and viruses.

Aptitude: A natural ability to do something or to learn something, often assessed to predict success in a given field or activity.

Area: The measure of the amount of space inside a two-dimensional boundary, often measured in square units.

Arithmetic: The branch of mathematics dealing with the properties and manipulation of numbers.

Arithmetic Reasoning (AR): A subtest of the ASVAB that measures the ability to solve arithmetic word problems.

Armor: Military vehicles equipped with heavy protection, such as tanks or armored personnel carriers.

Assembling Objects (AO): A subtest of the ASVAB that tests spatial relationship skills by requiring the determination of how an object will look when its parts are put together.

Assembly Language: A low-level programming language that uses symbolic code and is closely related to machine code.

ASVAB (Armed Services Vocational Aptitude Battery): A multiple-aptitude test used to measure strengths, weaknesses, and potential for future success in military and civilian occupations.

Asymptote: A line that continually approaches a given curve but does not meet it at any finite distance.

Atmosphere: The envelope of gases surrounding the earth or another planet.

Atom: The basic unit of a chemical element, consisting of a nucleus of protons and neutrons with electrons orbiting this nucleus.

Atomic Number: The number of protons in the nucleus of an atom, which determines the chemical properties of an element and its place in the periodic table.

Augment: To make something greater by adding to it; increase.

Aurora: A natural light display in the sky, typically seen in high-latitude regions, caused by the collision of energetic charged particles with atoms in the high-altitude atmosphere.

Auto and Shop Information (AS): A subtest of the ASVAB that assesses knowledge of automotive maintenance, repair, and wood and metal shop practices.

Axis: A reference line used in graphs and charts to indicate dimensions.

Accuracy: The degree to which a measurement or calculation conforms to the correct value or a standard.

B

Bandwidth: The range of frequencies within a given band, particularly that used for transmitting a signal.

Barometer: An instrument that measures atmospheric pressure, used especially in weather forecasting.

Barron's ASVAB: A comprehensive study guide that provides practice tests, subject reviews, and access to additional online practice for the ASVAB.

Base: The bottom support of anything; in mathematics, the number of different digits or combination of digits and letters that a system of counting uses to represent numbers.

Basic Training: The initial training program for new military personnel, teaching fundamental skills and knowledge.

Battery: A device consisting of one or more electrochemical cells that convert stored chemical energy into electrical energy.

Biodiversity: The variety of life in the world or in a particular habitat or ecosystem.

Biology: The study of living organisms, divided into many specialized fields.

Binary: A system of numerical notation that has 2 rather than 10 as a base.

Biotechnology: The exploitation of biological processes for industrial and other purposes, especially the genetic manipulation of microorganisms for the production of antibiotics, hormones, etc.

Boiling Point: The temperature at which a liquid turns to vapor.

Boolean Algebra: A branch of algebra in which the values of the variables are the truth values true and false, usually denoted 1 and 0 respectively, used in computer science and electrical engineering.

Botany: The scientific study of plants.

Buffer: A solution that can resist pH change upon the addition of an acidic or basic component.

Buoyancy: The ability or tendency of an object to float in water or other fluid.

Bureaucracy: A system of government in which most of the important decisions are made by state officials rather than by elected representatives.

Bullet: A projectile for firing from a rifle, revolver, or other small firearms, typically cylindrical and pointed, and sometimes containing an explosive.

Byproduct: A secondary product derived from a manufacturing process or chemical reaction.

Byte: A group of binary digits or bits (usually eight) operated on as a unit.

C

Celsius (°C): A scale and unit of measurement for temperature where 0°C is the freezing point of water and 100°C is its boiling point at standard atmospheric pressure.

Circuit: A closed path through which an electric current flows or may flow.

Climatology: The study of climate, scientifically defined as weather conditions averaged over a period of time.

Combustion: A chemical process in which a substance reacts rapidly with oxygen and gives off heat.

Composite Score: A score derived from the combination of various ASVAB subtest scores, used to qualify for specific military jobs.

Compression: The reduction in volume (causing an increase in pressure) of the fuel mixture in an internal combustion engine before ignition.

Conductivity: A measure of a material's ability to conduct an electric current.

Conductor: A material or object that permits an electric current to flow easily.

Conservation of Energy: A principle stating that energy cannot be created or destroyed, but can be altered from one form to another.

Constant: A quantity that remains the same throughout a given discussion or calculation.

Control Group: In scientific experimentation, the group that does not receive the experimental treatment, used as a benchmark to measure how the other tested subjects do.

Convection: The transfer of heat by the movement of a fluid (such as water or air) between areas of different temperature.

Coordinate Plane: A plane containing two perpendicular axes (x and y) intersecting at a point called the origin (0,0).

Current: The flow of electric charge in a conductor, measured in amperes (A).

Cytoplasm: The material within a living cell, excluding the nucleus.

Capacitance: The ability of a system to store an electric charge, measured in farads (F).

Catalyst: A substance that increases the rate of a chemical reaction without itself undergoing any permanent chemical change.

Cell Membrane: The semipermeable membrane surrounding the cytoplasm of a cell.

Chemical Bond: An attraction between atoms that allows the formation of chemical substances containing two or more atoms.

Chemical Reaction: A process that involves rearrangement of the molecular or ionic structure of a substance.

Chromosome: A thread-like structure of nucleic acids and protein found in the nucleus of most living cells, carrying genetic information in the form of genes.

Circulatory System: The system that circulates blood and lymph through the body, consisting of the heart, blood vessels, blood, lymph, and the lymphatic vessels and glands.

Coefficient: A numerical or constant quantity placed before and multiplying the variable in an algebraic expression (e.g., 4 in 4x).

Concentration: The abundance of a constituent divided by the total volume of a mixture.

Condensation: The process by which a vapor becomes a liquid; the opposite of evaporation.

Coulomb: The unit of electric charge in the International System of Units (SI), equal to the quantity of electricity conveyed in one second by a current of one ampere.

Critical Thinking: The objective analysis and evaluation of an issue in order to form a judgment.

Cross Product: A vector operation on two vectors in three-dimensional space, resulting in another vector that is perpendicular to the plane of the input vectors.

D

Data: Facts and statistics collected together for reference or analysis.

Database: An organized collection of data, generally stored and accessed electronically from a computer system.

DC (Direct Current): An electric current flowing in one direction only.

Decimal: A number that includes a decimal point followed by digits showing values less than one.

Decibel: A unit used to measure the intensity of a sound or the power level of an electrical signal by comparing it with a given level on a logarithmic scale.

Decompose: To break down a complex problem or system into smaller, more manageable parts.

Deduction: The process of reasoning from one or more statements (premises) to reach a logically certain conclusion.

Density: The mass of a substance per unit volume.

Desalination: The process of removing salt from seawater to produce fresh water.

Diagram: A simplified drawing showing the appearance, structure, or workings of something; a schematic representation.

Digital: Involving or relating to the use of computer technology.

Digital Signal: A signal that represents data as a sequence of discrete values.

Dimension: A measurable extent of some kind, such as length, breadth, depth, or height.

Diode: A semiconductor device with two terminals, typically allowing the flow of current in one direction only.

DNA (Deoxyribonucleic Acid): The carrier of genetic information in all living organisms.

Domain: A specified sphere of activity or knowledge.

Dosage: The size or frequency of a dose of a medicine or drug.

Drag: The force that opposes the motion of an object through a fluid (such as air or water).

Drill: A tool or machine with a rotating cutting tip or reciprocating hammer used for making holes.

Dynamic: Characterized by constant change, activity, or progress; in physics, it relates to forces producing motion.

Dynamo: A machine for converting mechanical energy into electrical energy; a generator.

E

Earth Science: The study of the earth and its atmosphere, including geology, meteorology, oceanography, and astronomy.

Ecology: The branch of biology that deals with the relationships between living organisms and their environment.

Efficiency: The ratio of useful output to total input, often expressed as a percentage, used to measure the effectiveness of machines and systems.

Electronics Information (EI): A subtest of the ASVAB that assesses knowledge of electrical circuits, systems, and electronic devices.

Element: A substance that cannot be broken down into simpler substances by chemical means, consisting of atoms with the same number of protons.

Elevation: The height above a given level, especially sea level.

Energy: The capacity to do work or produce heat, existing in various forms such as kinetic, potential, thermal, electrical, chemical, and nuclear.

Engineering: The application of scientific principles to design and build structures, machines, and other products, as well as to solve technical problems.

Entropy: A measure of the disorder or randomness in a system, often associated with the second law of thermodynamics.

Equilibrium: A state in which opposing forces or influences are balanced, often used in the context of chemical reactions and physical systems.

Erosion: The process by which soil, rock, or other surface material is worn away and removed by natural forces such as wind or water.

Evaporation: The process by which water changes from a liquid to a gas or vapor, often contributing to the water cycle.

Exothermic Reaction: A chemical reaction that releases energy in the form of heat.

Experiment: A scientific procedure undertaken to test a hypothesis by collecting data under controlled conditions.

Extinction: The dying out of a species, resulting in the permanent loss of its presence on Earth.

F

Fahrenheit: A temperature scale where the freezing point of water is 32 degrees and the boiling point is 212 degrees under standard atmospheric conditions.

Fiber Optics: The technology of transmitting light through thin, flexible fibers of glass or plastic to transmit data or information.

Force: In physics, a push or pull upon an object resulting from the object's interaction with another object, typically measured in newtons (N).

Frequency: The number of cycles per second of a periodic wave, measured in hertz (Hz).

Friction: The resistance that one surface or object encounters when moving over another.

Fuse: A safety device consisting of a strip of wire that melts and breaks an electric circuit if the current exceeds a safe level.

Fusion: A nuclear reaction in which atomic nuclei of low atomic number fuse to form a heavier nucleus with the release of energy.

Fuel Cell: A device that generates electricity by a chemical reaction, typically using hydrogen as a fuel.

Fulcrum: The support or point on which a lever pivots.

Function: In mathematics, a relation between a set of inputs and a set of permissible outputs with the property that each input is related to exactly one output.

Frequency Modulation (FM): A method of encoding data on a carrier wave by varying the frequency of the wave.

Frictional Force: The force exerted by a surface as an object moves across it or attempts to move across it.

Fuse (Electrical): A protective device used in electrical circuits to prevent excessive current flow, which could cause damage or fire.

Flight Dynamics: The study of the performance, stability, and control of vehicles flying through the air or in outer space.

Force (Mechanical): The interaction that, when unopposed, changes the motion of an object.

Frame of Reference: A coordinate system or set of axes within which to measure the position or movement of something.

G

G-Forces: The forces acting on a body as a result of acceleration or gravity, often experienced as a sensation of weight.

Galvanometer: An instrument for detecting and measuring electric current.

Gas: A state of matter characterized by having no fixed shape and no fixed volume.

Gauge: An instrument or device for measuring the magnitude, amount, or contents of something, typically with a visual display.

Genetics: The study of heredity and the variation of inherited characteristics.

Geology: The science that deals with the Earth's physical structure and substance, its history, and the processes that act on it.

Geometry: A branch of mathematics concerned with the properties and relations of points, lines, surfaces, solids, and higher-dimensional analogs.

Geyser: A hot spring in which water intermittently boils, sending a tall column of water and steam into the air.

Gigabyte: A unit of information equal to one billion (10^9) bytes.

Glacier: A slowly moving mass or river of ice formed by the accumulation and compaction of snow on mountains or near the poles.

Gravitational Force: The force of attraction between any two masses, particularly the attraction of the Earth's mass for bodies near its surface.

Grid: A network of lines that cross each other to form a series of squares or rectangles.

Ground State: The lowest energy state of an atom or other particle.

Gyroscope: A device used for measuring or maintaining orientation and angular velocity, typically consisting of a spinning wheel or disc.

Gyroscope Effect: The tendency of a spinning object to resist changes to its axis of rotation.

H

Half-life: The time required for a quantity to reduce to half its initial value. Commonly used in nuclear physics and chemistry to describe the decay of radioactive substances.

Halogen: Any of the elements fluorine, chlorine, bromine, iodine, and astatine, occupying group VIIA (17) of the periodic table. They are reactive nonmetallic elements that form strongly acidic compounds with hydrogen, from which simple salts can be made.

Harmonic: A wave whose frequency is a whole-number multiple of that of another. Used in physics to describe sound waves and vibrations.

Heat: A form of energy associated with the movement of atoms and molecules in any material. Heat is defined as the transfer of thermal energy across a well-defined boundary around a thermodynamic system.

Heat Capacity: The quantity of heat required to change a system's temperature by one degree. It is measured in joules per kelvin.

Heuristic: A practical approach to problem-solving that is not perfect but sufficient for the immediate goals. Often used in computer science and artificial intelligence.

Hertz (Hz): The unit of frequency in the International System of Units (SI), equal to one cycle per second.

Homeostasis: The tendency of a system, especially the physiological system of higher animals, to maintain internal stability.

Homogeneous: Of the same kind; alike. In chemistry, a homogeneous mixture has the same uniform appearance and composition throughout.

Hooke's Law: The principle that the force exerted by a spring is directly proportional to the amount it is stretched. Mathematically, $F = -kx$, where k is the spring constant and x is the displacement.

Hydraulic: Operated by, moved by, or employing water or other liquids in motion. Used in various machinery and equipment.

Hydrocarbon: An organic compound consisting entirely of hydrogen and carbon atoms. They are the principal constituents of petroleum and natural gas.

Hydrodynamics: The branch of science concerned with forces acting on or exerted by fluids (especially liquids).

Hydroelectric: Relating to the generation of electricity using flowing water to drive a turbine.

Hydrogen Bond: A weak bond between two molecules resulting from an electrostatic attraction between a proton in one molecule and an electronegative atom in the other.

Hydrology: The scientific study of the movement, distribution, and quality of water on Earth and other planets, including the water cycle, water resources, and environmental watershed sustainability.

Hypothesis: A proposed explanation for a phenomenon, serving as the basis for further investigation.

Hysteresis: The lag in response exhibited by a body in reacting to changes in the forces, especially magnetic forces, affecting it. Often observed in physical systems where the effect of the force is delayed.

I

IC (Integrated Circuit): A set of electronic circuits on one small flat piece (or "chip") of semiconductor material, normally silicon.

Induction: The process or action of bringing about or giving rise to something.

Inference: A conclusion reached on the basis of evidence and reasoning.

Insulation: Material used to prevent the passage of electricity, heat, or sound from one conductor to another.

Ion: An atom or molecule with a net electric charge due to the loss or gain of one or more electrons.

IR (Infrared Radiation): Electromagnetic radiation with wavelengths longer than visible light but shorter than radio waves.

Isotope: Variants of a particular chemical element that have different numbers of neutrons.

Itinerary: A planned route or journey.

Intuition: The ability to understand something immediately, without the need for conscious reasoning.

Inertia: The resistance of any physical object to any change in its state of motion; this includes changes to the object's speed, direction, or state of rest.

Integrity: The quality of being honest and having strong moral principles.

Intrinsic: Belonging naturally; essential.

ISO (International Organization for Standardization): An international standard-setting body composed of representatives from various national standards organizations.

Iteration: The repetition of a process or set of instructions in a computer program.

Impedance: The effective resistance of an electric circuit or component to alternating current, arising from the combined effects of ohmic resistance and reactance.

J

Job Placements: The assignment of military personnel to specific roles based on their ASVAB scores and qualifications.

Joint Operation: A military action conducted by multiple service branches working together.

Joule: A unit of energy in the International System of Units (SI), symbolized as J, equivalent to the energy transferred when applying a force of one newton over a distance of one meter.

Judgment: The ability to make considered decisions or come to sensible conclusions.

Junction: A point where two or more things are joined, such as electrical circuits or pathways.

Justification: The action of showing something to be right or reasonable; in math, the reasoning behind solving a problem in a particular way.

Jitter: Small, rapid variations in a waveform resulting from fluctuations in the signal's timing, often seen in electronics and communications.

Jet Stream: Fast flowing, narrow air currents found in the atmospheres of some planets, including Earth.

Jargon: Special words or expressions used by a profession or group that are difficult for others to understand.

Job Corps: A free education and training program that helps young people learn a career, earn a high school diploma or GED, and find and keep a good job.

Job Analysis: The process of gathering, documenting, and analyzing information about the responsibilities and the context of a specific job.

Jigsaw Puzzle: A tiling puzzle that requires the assembly of often oddly shaped interlocking and tessellating pieces. Each piece usually has a small part of a picture on it; when complete, a jigsaw puzzle produces a complete picture.

Joint Chiefs of Staff: The body of senior uniformed leaders in the United States Department of Defense who advise the President of the United States, the Secretary of Defense, the Homeland Security Council, and the National Security Council on military matters.

Jump Start: To start a vehicle by temporarily connecting the battery to another power source or battery.

Junction Box: An enclosure housing electrical connections, to protect the connections and provide a safety barrier.

Jurisprudence: The theory or philosophy of law.

Jurisdiction: The official power to make legal decisions and judgments, often in specific areas or over certain issues.

K

Kilogram: The basic unit of mass in the metric system, equivalent to 1,000 grams.

Kinetic Energy: The energy possessed by an object due to its motion, calculated as $\frac{1}{2}mv^2$ where m is mass and v is velocity.

Kirchhoff's Laws: A set of rules for analyzing complex electrical circuits, including Kirchhoff's Current Law (the total current entering a junction equals the total current leaving) and Kirchhoff's Voltage Law (the sum of all voltages around a closed loop equals zero).

Knot: A unit of speed equal to one nautical mile per hour, commonly used in maritime and aviation contexts.

Knowledge: Information and skills acquired through experience or education; the theoretical or practical understanding of a subject.

Keystone Species: A species on which other species in an ecosystem largely depend, such that if it were removed the ecosystem would change drastically.

Kinematics: The branch of physics that deals with the motion of objects without considering the forces that cause the motion.

Kilowatt: A unit of power equal to 1,000 watts, often used to measure the output of engines and the power consumption of appliances.

Kilo- (prefix): A prefix in the metric system denoting a factor of 1,000.

Kinetic Friction: The force that opposes the relative motion of two contacting surfaces that are in motion with respect to each other.

Knot Theory: A branch of topology that studies mathematical knots, their properties, and their applications.

L

Latitude: The measurement of distance north or south of the Equator, expressed in degrees.

Lever: A simple machine consisting of a beam or rigid rod pivoted at a fixed hinge, or fulcrum, used to transfer force and motion.

Line: In geometry, a straight one-dimensional figure having no thickness and extending infinitely in both directions.

Line Segment: A part of a line that is bounded by two distinct end points, and contains every point on the line between its endpoints.

Logarithm: The exponent or power to which a base, usually 10 or e, must be raised to produce a given number.

Longitude: The measurement of distance east or west of the prime meridian, expressed in degrees.

Lubrication: The application of a substance (like oil or grease) to minimize friction and wear between surfaces in contact.

Luster: The way a mineral reflects light from its surface; can be metallic or non-metallic.

Lymphatic System: The network of vessels through which lymph drains from the tissues into the blood, playing a key role in immune response.

Load: The weight or force that is supported by a structure, component, or material.

Lift: An aerodynamic force that holds an aircraft in the air, counteracting gravity.

Life Cycle: The series of changes in the life of an organism, including reproduction.

Lignite: A soft brownish coal showing traces of plant structure, intermediate between bituminous coal and peat.

Lantern: A transparent or translucent case for enclosing a light and protecting it from the wind and weather.

Lock: A mechanical device used to secure an object or area, typically operated by a key or combination.

Laser: A device that generates an intense beam of coherent monochromatic light (or other electromagnetic radiation) by stimulated emission of photons from excited atoms or molecules.

Lathe: A machine tool used to shape a piece of material by rotating it rapidly along its axis while applying various tools to perform operations such as cutting, sanding, drilling, or deformation.

Lateral: Relating to the side of something.

Lever Arm: The perpendicular distance from the axis of rotation to the line of action of the force.

Lattice: A regular, repeating arrangement of points in space, often used to describe the arrangement of atoms in a crystal.

Limiting Reactant: The substance that is totally consumed when the chemical reaction is complete, limiting the amount of product formed.

Load-Bearing: Referring to a structure or component that supports the weight of other elements above it.

M

Magnetism: A physical phenomenon produced by the motion of electric charge, resulting in attractive and repulsive forces between objects.

Mains Electricity: The general-purpose alternating-current (AC) electric power supply.

Mass: A measure of the amount of matter in an object, typically measured in kilograms or grams.

Matter: Anything that has mass and takes up space, consisting of atoms and molecules.

Mechanical Advantage: The ratio of the force produced by a machine to the force applied to it, used in assessing the performance of a machine.

Mechanical Comprehension (MC): A subtest of the ASVAB that measures understanding of mechanical and physical principles.

Mechanics: The branch of physics dealing with the motion of objects and the forces that affect them.

Metabolism: The set of life-sustaining chemical reactions in organisms.

Meteorology: The scientific study of the atmosphere that focuses on weather processes and forecasting.

Microscope: An optical instrument used for viewing very small objects, such as mineral samples or biological cells.

Mil: A unit of angular measurement equal to 1/6400 of a complete revolution, used in artillery.

Military Occupational Specialty (MOS): The specific job or career field a service member is trained to perform in the Army and Marine Corps.

Mitosis: A process of cell division that results in two genetically identical daughter cells.

Momentum: The quantity of motion an object has, dependent on its mass and velocity.

Motor: A machine, especially one powered by electricity or internal combustion, that supplies motive power for a vehicle or for some other device with moving parts.

Mutual Inductance: The principle where two inductors induce voltage in each other.

Myopia: Nearsightedness; a condition where close objects appear clearly, but distant ones do not.

N

Navy: One of the branches of the United States Armed Forces, primarily responsible for naval and maritime operations.

Neutron: A subatomic particle found in the nucleus of an atom, with no electrical charge.

Newton's Laws: Three fundamental principles that describe the relationship between the motion of an object and the forces acting on it.

Node: A point in a network or diagram where lines or pathways intersect or branch.

Nominal: Refers to a value or designation in name only, often used in engineering to describe a standard size or measurement that may not be precise.

Nonrenewable Resource: A natural resource that cannot be replenished or takes millions of years to form, such as fossil fuels.

Normal Distribution: A probability distribution that is symmetrical around the mean, often represented as a bell curve.

Nucleus: The central and most important part of an atom, containing protons and neutrons.

Nutrient: A substance that provides nourishment essential for growth and the maintenance of life.

Nyquist Theorem: A principle that specifies the minimum rate at which a signal can be sampled without introducing errors, important in the field of digital signal processing.

O

Observation: The act of noting and recording an event, characteristic, or behavior in a systematic way.

Ohm (Ω): The unit of electrical resistance in the International System of Units (SI). One ohm is equal to the resistance that produces a potential difference of one volt when a current of one ampere is flowing through it.

Ohm's Law: A fundamental principle of electricity stating that the current (I) passing through a conductor between two points is directly proportional to the voltage (V) across the two points and inversely proportional to the resistance (R) between them. It is often written as $V = IR$.

Olfactory: Relating to the sense of smell.

Oncology: The branch of medicine that deals with the prevention, diagnosis, and treatment of cancer.

Optics: The branch of physics that deals with the behavior and properties of light, including its interactions with matter and the construction of instruments that use or detect it.

Orbit: The curved path of a celestial object or spacecraft around a star, planet, or moon, especially a periodic elliptical revolution.

Ornithology: The scientific study of birds.

Oscillation: Movement back and forth at a regular speed.

Oscilloscope: An electronic device used to display and analyze the waveform of electronic signals. It provides a graphical representation of voltage as a function of time.

Osmosis: The movement of solvent molecules through a semi-permeable membrane from a region of lower solute concentration to a region of higher solute concentration, aiming to equalize concentrations on both sides of the membrane.

Oxidation: A chemical reaction in which a substance loses electrons, often associated with gaining oxygen or losing hydrogen. It is part of redox (reduction-oxidation) reactions where one substance is oxidized and another is reduced.

Oxidizing Agent: A substance that has the ability to oxidize other substances, in other words, to accept their electrons.

Oxygen: A chemical element with the symbol O and atomic number 8. It is essential for respiration in most living organisms and is a part of the Earth's atmosphere.

Ozone (O₃): A molecule composed of three oxygen atoms. It is found in the Earth's stratosphere and absorbs the majority of the sun's harmful ultraviolet radiation.

Ozone Layer: A layer in the Earth's stratosphere containing a high concentration of ozone, which absorbs most of the ultraviolet radiation reaching the Earth from the sun.

Outer Core: The layer of the Earth located beneath the mantle and above the inner core. It is composed of liquid iron and nickel and is responsible for generating the Earth's magnetic field.

Overhead Camshaft (OHC): An engine configuration in which the camshaft is located above the cylinder head, often resulting in better performance and higher efficiency in internal combustion engines.

Overhead Valve (OHV): An engine design where the intake and exhaust valves are located in the cylinder head above the piston, often referred to in automotive contexts.

P

Parallel Circuit: An electrical circuit in which the components are connected in parallel, meaning the current divides into two or more paths before recombining to complete the circuit.

Parallel Lines: Lines in a plane that do not intersect or meet, no matter how far they are extended.

Parasitology: The study of parasites and their interactions with their hosts.

Pascal (Pa): The SI unit of pressure, equal to one newton per square meter.

Pathogen: An organism that causes disease, such as bacteria, viruses, fungi, or parasites.

Pendulum: A weight suspended from a pivot so that it can swing freely, often used in clocks.

Perimeter: The continuous line forming the boundary of a closed geometric figure.

Periodic Table: A table of the chemical elements arranged in order of atomic number, typically in rows so that elements with similar atomic structure (and hence similar chemical properties) appear in vertical columns.

Peristalsis: The series of wave-like muscle contractions that moves food through the digestive tract.

Petrology: The branch of geology that studies rocks and the conditions under which they form.

pH: A measure of the acidity or alkalinity of a solution, ranging from 0 to 14, with 7 being neutral. Lower numbers indicate acidity, and higher numbers indicate alkalinity.

Phagocytosis: The process by which a cell engulfs particles such as bacteria, other microorganisms, or cellular debris.

Pharmacology: The branch of medicine and biology concerned with the study of drug action.

Phenotype: The set of observable characteristics of an individual resulting from the interaction of its genotype with the environment.

Photon: A particle representing a quantum of light or other electromagnetic radiation.

Photosynthesis: The process by which green plants and some other organisms use sunlight to synthesize foods with the aid of chlorophyll.

Physical Change: A change in which no new substances are formed, such as melting, freezing, and boiling.

Physics: The natural science that studies matter, energy, and the fundamental forces of nature, and how they interact.

Pigment: A substance that gives color to tissue.

Plate Tectonics: The theory in geology that explains the movement of the Earth's lithosphere which is divided into tectonic plates.

Pollination: The transfer of pollen from the male part of a plant to the female part of a plant, allowing fertilization to take place.

Polymer: A large molecule composed of many repeated subunits (monomers).

Potential Energy: The energy possessed by an object because of its position relative to other objects, internal stresses, electric charge, or other factors.

Precipitation: Any form of water - liquid or solid - falling from the sky, including rain, sleet, snow, and hail.

Prokaryote: A single-celled organism without a nucleus, such as bacteria and archaea.

Protein Synthesis: The process by which cells build proteins based on the instructions in genes.

Proton: A subatomic particle with a positive electric charge found in the nucleus of an atom.

Pulley: A simple machine consisting of a wheel over which a rope or belt is pulled to lift or lower a load.

Q

Quadratic Equation: A second-order polynomial equation in a single variable with the form $ax^2 + bx + c = 0$, where a, b and c are constants.

Quadrant: One of the four sections of the coordinate plane divided by the x-axis and y-axis.

Qualitative Data: Information that describes qualities or characteristics and is often collected using observations or interviews. This data is non-numerical.

Quantitative Data: Information that can be measured and written down with numbers. This type of data includes quantities, amounts, or ranges.

Quantum Mechanics: The branch of physics that deals with the behavior of very small particles, typically atoms and subatomic particles, where the principles of classical mechanics no longer apply.

Quantum Theory: The theoretical basis of modern physics explaining the nature and behavior of matter and energy on the atomic and subatomic level.

Quark: A fundamental constituent of matter observed in protons and neutrons, which combine to form hadrons. Quarks are held together by the strong force.

Quartz: A hard, crystalline mineral composed of silicon and oxygen atoms, commonly found in the Earth's crust.

Quasar: An extremely luminous and distant active galactic nucleus, powered by a supermassive black hole at its center.

Quarantine: A period of isolation imposed on people, animals, or plants to prevent the spread of disease or pests.

Quark-Gluon Plasma: A state of matter in quantum chromodynamics (QCD) which exists at extremely high temperature and/or density, consisting of free quarks and gluons.

Quasi-Experimental Design: A type of research design that seeks to establish a cause-and-effect relationship but lacks the random assignment of participants to experimental and control groups found in true experiments.

Quaternary Structure: The fourth level of protein structure, involving the association of multiple polypeptide chains into a functional protein complex.

Quiescent: In a state or period of inactivity or dormancy.

Quota: A fixed share or number of something that a person or group is entitled to receive or is bound to contribute.

R

Radiation: The emission of energy as electromagnetic waves or as moving subatomic particles, especially high-energy particles that cause ionization.

Radioactive Decay: The process by which an unstable atomic nucleus loses energy by emitting radiation.

Radiocarbon Dating: A method for determining the age of an object containing organic material by measuring the properties of radiocarbon (carbon-14).

Radius: The distance from the center of a circle to any point on its circumference.

Reactant: A substance that takes part in and undergoes change during a reaction.

Reaction Rate: The speed at which a chemical reaction proceeds, typically expressed in terms of the concentration of a reactant consumed or product formed per unit time.

Receptor: A protein molecule that receives chemical signals from outside a cell.

Red Blood Cell: A type of blood cell that is responsible for carrying oxygen from the lungs to the rest of the body and returning carbon dioxide to the lungs to be exhaled.

Reduction: A chemical reaction that involves the gaining of electrons by one of the atoms involved in the reaction.

Refraction: The bending of light as it passes from one medium to another medium of different density.

Regeneration: The process of renewal, restoration, and growth that makes genomes, cells, organisms, and ecosystems resilient to natural fluctuations or events that cause disturbance or damage.

Relative Humidity: The amount of moisture in the air compared to what the air can hold at that temperature, expressed as a percentage.

Renewable Energy: Energy from a source that is not depleted when used, such as wind or solar power.

Reproduction: The biological process by which new individual organisms are produced.

Resistance (Electrical): A measure of the degree to which a conductor opposes an electric current through that conductor.

Respiration: The process in which organisms exchange gases with their environment, typically taking in oxygen and releasing carbon dioxide.

RNA (Ribonucleic Acid): A nucleic acid present in all living cells that acts as a messenger carrying instructions from DNA for controlling the synthesis of proteins.

Rocket Propulsion: The act of driving or propelling a rocket forward by expelling gas at high speed from a rocket engine.

Rotation: The action of rotating around an axis or center.

Rough Endoplasmic Reticulum (RER): A type of endoplasmic reticulum that is studded with ribosomes and involved in the synthesis of proteins.

Ruminant: A mammal that chews cud regurgitated from its rumen. Examples include cattle, sheep, and goats.

Rutherford Model: A model of the atom devised by Ernest Rutherford in which an atom consists of a central, positively charged nucleus surrounded by electrons.

S

Satellite: An artificial body placed in orbit around the earth or moon or another planet in order to collect information or for communication.

Scalar: A physical quantity that has magnitude but no direction, such as mass or temperature.

Sedimentary Rock: Type of rock that is formed by the accumulation or deposition of mineral or organic particles at the Earth's surface, followed by cementation.

Seismograph: An instrument that measures and records details of earthquakes, such as force and duration.

Series Circuit: An electric circuit in which the components are connected end-to-end so that the current flows through each component one after another.

Simple Machine: A mechanical device that changes the direction or magnitude of a force. Common examples include levers, pulleys, and inclined planes.

Solstice: Either of the two times in the year, the summer solstice and the winter solstice, when the sun reaches its highest or lowest point in the sky at noon, marked by the longest and shortest days.

Solution: A homogeneous mixture composed of two or more substances. In a solution, a solute is dissolved in a solvent.

Solvent: The substance in which the solute dissolves in a solution.

Species: The basic unit of biological classification and a taxonomic rank, as well as a unit of biodiversity. A species is often defined as a group of organisms that can reproduce with one another in nature and produce fertile offspring.

Specific Heat: The amount of heat required to raise the temperature of one gram of a substance by one degree Celsius.

Spectrum: A band of colors, as seen in a rainbow, produced by separation of the components of light by their different degrees of refraction according to wavelength.

Speed: The distance traveled per unit of time.

Spore: A reproductive cell capable of developing into a new individual without fusion with another reproductive cell. Spores are produced by bacteria, fungi, algae, and plants.

Static Electricity: A stationary electric charge, typically produced by friction, that causes sparks or crackling or the attraction of dust or hair.

Stratosphere: The layer of the earth's atmosphere above the troposphere, extending to about 50 km (31 miles) above the earth's surface.

Symbiosis: Interaction between two different organisms living in close physical association, typically to the advantage of both.

Synthesis: The production of chemical compounds by reaction from simpler materials.

Systolic Pressure: The blood pressure when the heart is contracting. It is the first number recorded in a blood pressure reading.

Systemic Circulation: The part of the cardiovascular system which carries oxygenated blood away from the heart to the body, and returns deoxygenated blood back to the heart.

Systemic System: The set of interacting or interdependent components, real or abstract, that form an integrated whole.

These terms cover essential concepts that may appear in the ASVAB, providing a strong foundation in various subjects tested in the exam.

T

Tachometer: An instrument that measures the rotational speed of a shaft or disk, as in a motor or other machine.

Tangent: In trigonometry, a tangent of an angle is the ratio of the length of the opposite side to the length of the adjacent side in a right-angled triangle.

Taxonomy: The science of classification of organisms in an ordered system that indicates natural relationships.

Temperature: A measure of the warmth or coldness of an object or substance with reference to some standard value.

Tension: The state of being stretched tight, often used to describe the force exerted by a cable or rope when it is pulled tight by forces acting from opposite ends.

Terminal Velocity: The constant speed that a freely falling object eventually reaches when the resistance of the medium through which it is falling prevents further acceleration.

Thermodynamics: The branch of physical science that deals with the relations between heat and other forms of energy.

Tissue: An ensemble of similar cells and their extracellular matrix from the same origin that together carry out a specific function.

Torque: A measure of the force that can cause an object to rotate about an axis.

Transcription: The process of copying a segment of DNA into RNA.

Transformer: An electrical device that transfers electrical energy between two or more circuits through electromagnetic induction.

Translation (Biology): The process in which cellular ribosomes create proteins, following transcription of DNA to RNA in the cell's nucleus.

Transpiration: The process by which moisture is carried through plants from roots to small pores on the underside of leaves, where it changes to vapor and is released to the atmosphere.

Trophic Level: Each of several hierarchical levels in an ecosystem, comprising organisms that share the same function in the food chain and the same nutritional relationship to the primary sources of energy.

Tropism: The growth or movement of an organism in response to an environmental stimulus such as light (phototropism) or gravity (gravitropism).

Tsunami: A long high sea wave caused by an earthquake, submarine landslide, or other disturbance.

Tundra: A type of biome where the tree growth is hindered by low temperatures and short growing seasons.

Turbine: A machine for producing continuous power in which a wheel or rotor, typically fitted with vanes, is made to revolve by a fast-moving flow of water, steam, gas, air, or other fluid.

Twilight: The time of day immediately following sunset or preceding sunrise, characterized by a diffused light before it becomes completely dark or light.

Tympanic Membrane: Also known as the eardrum, it is a thin membrane that separates the external ear from the middle ear and transmits sound vibrations to the ossicles of the middle ear.

These terms cover essential concepts that may appear in the ASVAB, providing a strong foundation in various subjects tested in the exam.

U

Ultrasound: Sound or other vibrations having an ultrasonic frequency, particularly as used in medical imaging.

Ultraviolet (UV) Radiation: A form of electromagnetic radiation with a wavelength shorter than that of visible light but longer than X-rays. UV radiation is known for its ability to cause sunburn and is used in sterilization processes.

Unbalanced Force: Forces that cause a change in the motion of an object. An unbalanced force results when the sum of the forces acting on an object is not zero.

Unicellular: Consisting of a single cell. Examples include bacteria and protozoa.

Universal Gravitation: Newton's law that states that every mass attracts every other mass in the universe, and the force between two masses is proportional to the product of their masses and inversely proportional to the square of the distance between their centers.

Universe: All of space and everything in it including stars, planets, galaxies, etc. The universe is all of time and space and its contents.

Unsaturated Solution: A solution that contains less solute than it has the capacity to dissolve at a given temperature.

Uplift: The process by which regions of the Earth's crust are raised to higher elevations due to tectonic forces.

Uranium: A heavy, silvery-white, toxic, metallic, and naturally radioactive chemical element with symbol U and atomic number 92. Uranium is used as a fuel in nuclear reactors.

Urbanization: The process by which an increasing percentage of a population lives in cities and suburbs. This process often accompanies industrialization.

Urinary System: The body's drainage system for removing urine, which includes the kidneys, ureters, bladder, and urethra.

Urology: The branch of medicine and physiology concerned with the function and disorders of the urinary system.

Usability: The ease of use and learnability of a human-made object such as a tool or device. Usability can also refer to the methods of measuring the usability and studying the principles behind an object's perceived efficiency.

User Interface (UI): The means by which the user and a computer system interact, in particular the use of input devices and software.

Utility: In economics, the measure of preferences over some set of goods and services. Utility represents satisfaction experienced by the consumer.

Utopia: An imagined community or society that possesses highly desirable or nearly perfect qualities for its citizens.

V

Vacuum: A space entirely devoid of matter, where the pressure is significantly lower than atmospheric pressure.

Valence Electrons: The electrons in the outermost shell of an atom that are involved in forming bonds with other atoms.

Vascular Plant: A plant that has specialized tissues (xylem and phloem) for transporting water, nutrients, and photosynthetic products throughout the plant.

Velocity: The speed of something in a given direction. It is a vector quantity, meaning it has both magnitude and direction.

Venous System: The network of veins that return deoxygenated blood to the heart.

Venn Diagram: A diagram that uses circles to represent the relationships among different sets or groups, showing where they overlap and where they differ.

Ventricle: One of the two lower chambers of the heart that pumps blood out to the arteries.

Vertebrate: An animal of a large group distinguished by the possession of a backbone or spinal column, including mammals, birds, reptiles, amphibians, and fish.

Vertical Integration: The combination in one company of two or more stages of production normally operated by separate companies.

Virus: A small infectious agent that replicates only inside the living cells of an organism. Viruses can infect all types of life forms, from animals and plants to microorganisms.

Viscosity: A measure of a fluid's resistance to flow. Higher viscosity means the fluid flows less easily.

Vitamin: Any of a group of organic compounds that are essential for normal growth and nutrition and are required in small quantities in the diet because they cannot be synthesized by the body.

Volt (V): The derived unit for electric potential, electric potential difference, and electromotive force. It is the potential difference between two points of a conducting wire carrying a constant current of one ampere when the power dissipated between these points is one watt.

Voltage: The electric potential difference between two points, which drives the flow of electric current in a circuit.

Voltmeter: An instrument for measuring electric potential difference between two points in an electric circuit.

Volume: The amount of space that a substance or object occupies, or that is enclosed within a container, especially when great.

Voluntary Muscle: Muscle that is under conscious control, such as skeletal muscles.

Vortex: A region within a fluid where the flow is predominantly rotational. Examples include whirlpools in water and tornadoes in air.

Vulcanization: A chemical process for converting rubber or related polymers into more durable materials by the addition of sulfur or other equivalent curatives or accelerators.

W

Watt (W): The unit of power in the International System of Units (SI), equivalent to one joule per second. It measures the rate of energy transfer.

Wavelength: The distance between successive crests of a wave, especially points in a sound wave or electromagnetic wave.

Weathering: The process by which rocks and minerals are broken down, physically and chemically, by the action of wind, water, and biological activity.

Weir: A barrier built across a river to control the flow of water, often used to measure discharge.

Weight: The force exerted on a body by gravity, calculated as the mass of the body times the local acceleration due to gravity.

Wetland: A land area that is saturated with water, either permanently or seasonally, such that it takes on the characteristics of a distinct ecosystem.

Wheel and Axle: A simple machine consisting of a wheel attached to a smaller cylindrical drum (axle), used to amplify force.

White Blood Cell: A type of blood cell that is involved in the body's immune response, helping to fight infection.

Wind Chill: The lowering of body temperature due to the passing-flow of lower-temperature air. It is the perceived decrease in air temperature felt by the body on exposed skin due to the flow of air.

Wind Turbine: A device that converts kinetic energy from the wind into electrical power.

Work: In physics, work is defined as the energy transferred to or from an object via the application of force along a displacement. It is calculated as $\text{Work} = \text{Force} \times \text{Distance}$

Worm Gear: A mechanical arrangement consisting of a spirally threaded shaft (worm) that engages with and drives a toothed wheel (gear).

Wristwatch: A small timepiece worn typically on a strap around the wrist.

Wrought Iron: A form of iron that is tough, malleable, and can be welded, used especially for decorative fences, gates, and furniture.

X

X-Axis: The horizontal axis in a coordinate system, typically used to represent the independent variable in a graph.

X-Chromosome: One of the two sex chromosomes in humans and many other organisms. Females have two X chromosomes, while males have one X and one Y chromosome.

X-Ray: A form of electromagnetic radiation with a wavelength shorter than ultraviolet light but longer than gamma rays. X-rays are used in medical imaging to view inside the body and in various industrial applications for inspecting materials.

Xerophyte: A plant adapted to grow in dry conditions with features such as thick, fleshy leaves or stems that store water.

Xylem: The vascular tissue in plants that conducts water and dissolved nutrients upward from the roots to the rest of the plant and also helps to form the woody element in the stem.

Xenon (Xe): A chemical element with the symbol Xe and atomic number 54. It is a colorless, dense, odorless noble gas found in the Earth's atmosphere in trace amounts and used in certain specialized lighting and medical applications.

Xerography: A dry photocopying technique invented by Chester Carlson in 1938, commonly used in copy machines and laser printers.

Xenotransplantation: The transplantation of living cells, tissues, or organs from one species to another, such as from pigs to humans.

Xenobiotic: A chemical substance that is foreign to the biological system. This term is often used in the context of environmental pollution and toxicology.

Y

Y-Axis: The vertical axis in a coordinate system, typically used to represent the dependent variable in a graph.

Y-Chromosome: One of the two sex chromosomes in humans and many other organisms. Males have one Y chromosome and one X chromosome, while females have two X chromosomes. The Y chromosome is responsible for determining male sex characteristics.

Yeast: A type of fungus used in baking and brewing. Yeast ferments sugars, producing carbon dioxide and alcohol, which causes bread to rise and produces alcoholic beverages.

Yellow Dwarf: A small, yellow star like our sun. It is in a stable phase of its life cycle, burning hydrogen into helium in its core.

Yield: In chemistry, yield refers to the amount of product obtained from a chemical reaction. It can be expressed as a percentage of the theoretical maximum amount of product that could be formed from the reactants.

Yolk: The nutrient-rich portion of an egg, which feeds the developing embryo in egg-laying animals.

Young's Modulus: A measure of the ability of a material to withstand changes in length when under lengthwise tension or compression. It is a measure of the stiffness of a solid material.

Yotta- (Y): The prefix in the International System of Units (SI) representing $1024 \cdot 10^{24} \cdot 1024$. For example, one yottabyte is $1024 \cdot 10^{24} \cdot 1024$ bytes.

Ytterbium (Yb): A chemical element with the symbol Yb and atomic number 70. It is a soft, malleable, and ductile rare earth element used in various high-tech applications such as lasers and certain types of steel.

Yttrium (Y): A chemical element with the symbol Y and atomic number 39. It is a transition metal often used in the production of phosphors, which are used in television and computer screens, and in various high-temperature superconductors.

Z

Z-Axis: The axis in a three-dimensional coordinate system that is usually oriented vertically and represents the third dimension in addition to the x-axis and y-axis.

Zener Diode: A type of diode designed to allow current to flow in the reverse direction when a specific, predetermined voltage is reached. It is commonly used for voltage regulation.

Zinc (Zn): A chemical element with the symbol Zn and atomic number 30. Zinc is a metal used to galvanize steel, in making alloys, and as a dietary supplement.

Zirconium (Zr): A chemical element with the symbol Zr and atomic number 40. Zirconium is used in nuclear reactors due to its low absorption cross-section for thermal neutrons.

Zoology: The scientific study of animals, including their biology, physiology, structure, genetics, and classification.

Zygote: The initial cell formed when two gamete cells are joined by means of sexual reproduction. It contains the complete set of chromosomes and is the first stage of embryonic development.

Zero Gravity: The condition of apparent weightlessness experienced in free fall or in an environment without a gravitational pull, such as space.

Zone of Saturation: The area below the water table where all open spaces in sediment and rock are completely filled with water.

Zooplankton: Small floating or weakly swimming animals that drift with water currents and form a fundamental part of the aquatic food web.

Zygomatic Bone: Also known as the cheekbone or malar bone, it is a paired bone that articulates with the maxilla, temporal bone, sphenoid bone, and frontal bone, forming the prominence of the cheek.

Additional Study Resources

To further aid your preparation for the ASVAB, consider utilizing the following official resources:

1. **Official ASVAB Website**: The official ASVAB website (**www.officialasvab.com**) offers a wealth of information, including detailed descriptions of the test sections, practice questions, and study tips. This site is an essential resource for understanding the test format and what to expect on exam day.

2. **Department of Defense's ASVAB Program**: The ASVAB Career Exploration Program (**www.asvabprogram.com**) provides tools to help you understand your skills and interests, explore careers, and develop a plan for your future. It includes practice tests and career exploration tools that can help you prepare effectively.

3. **Military Branches' Recruitment Websites**: Each branch of the U.S. Armed Forces provides resources specific to their recruitment processes, including information about the ASVAB. Visit the official websites of the Army, Navy, Air Force, Marine Corps, and Coast Guard for branch-specific information and resources.

4. **Official ASVAB Practice Tests**: Utilize the official ASVAB practice tests available on the official ASVAB website or through the ASVAB Career Exploration Program. These practice tests will give you a realistic sense of the exam structure and the types of questions you will encounter.

5. **U.S. Military Entrance Processing Command (USMEPCOM)**: The USMEPCOM website (**www.mepcom.army.mil**) provides information about the enlistment process, including details about the ASVAB. This resource is valuable for understanding the logistical aspects of taking the test and what happens after you receive your scores.

Moreover, you can incorporate a variety of reputable resources that cover the key subject areas tested on the exam. Here's a suggested bibliography of materials you can use:

1. Khan Academy (**www.khanacademy.org**): While not specifically designed for the ASVAB, this free educational platform offers excellent resources for math, science, and other subjects covered in the test.

2. Grammar Hero YouTube channel: This resource is highly recommended for its step-by-step explanations of math concepts, from basic to more complex, and includes practice tests that closely resemble the actual ASVAB

3. Engineering Explained YouTube Channel: Provides in-depth explanations of automotive technology and engineering concepts.

These resources will provide you with accurate, reliable, and comprehensive information to help you prepare effectively for the ASVAB. Make sure to utilize these tools to complement your study efforts and enhance your readiness for the exam.

By using this glossary and study resources you can further enhance your preparation for the ASVAB and maximize your chances of achieving a high score. The additional resources will provide you with more practice opportunities and insights, while the glossary and index will help you navigate the material more efficiently. Good luck on your ASVAB journey!

Bibliography

General Science Study Books

1. **Gibilisco, Stan.** *Teach Yourself Electricity and Electronics.* 7th ed., McGraw-Hill Education, 2016.

2. **Sclar, Deanna.** *Auto Repair For Dummies.* 2nd ed., For Dummies, 2019.

3. **Newton, Tom.** *How Cars Work.* Black Apple Press, 1999.

Arithmetic Books

1. **Lang, Serge.** *Basic Mathematics.* Springer, 1988.

2. **Kelley, W. Michael.** *The Humongous Book of Basic Math and Pre-Algebra Problems.* Alpha, 2010.

3. **Gibilisco, Stan.** *Teach Yourself Electricity and Electronics.* 7th ed., McGraw-Hill Education, 2016.

Electronics Information

1. **Gibilisco, Stan.** *Teach Yourself Electricity and Electronics.* 7th ed., McGraw-Hill Education, 2016.

2. **Scharf, Steven.** *Electronics For Dummies.* For Dummies, 2012.

3. **Scherz, Paul, and Simon Monk.** *Practical Electronics for Inventors.* 4th ed., McGraw-Hill Education, 2016.

Mechanical Comprehension

1. **McMunn, Richard.** *Mechanical Comprehension Tests: Sample Test Questions and Answers.* How2Become Ltd, 2013.

2. **Bailey, Chris.** *The Productivity Project: Accomplishing More by Managing Your Time, Attention, and Energy.* Crown Business, 2016.

3. **Halderman, James D.** *Automotive Technology: Principles, Diagnosis, and Service.* 5th ed., Pearson, 2015.

Auto and Shop Information

1. **Sclar, Deanna.** *Auto Repair For Dummies.* 2nd ed., For Dummies, 2019.

2. **Duffy, James E.** *Modern Automotive Technology.* 9th ed., Goodheart-Willcox, 2017.

3. **Molla, Tony.** *The Complete Idiot's Guide to Auto Repair.* Alpha, 2007.

Spatial Awareness

1. **Sorby, Sheryl.** *Developing Spatial Thinking.* Cengage Learning, 2017.
2. **Yenawine, Philip.** *Visual Thinking Strategies: Using Art to Deepen Learning Across School Disciplines.* Harvard Education Press, 2013.
3. **Platt, Charles.** *Make: Electronics: Learning by Discovery.* 2nd ed., Maker Media, Inc., 2015.

Verbal Proficiency

1. **Lewis, Norman.** *Word Power Made Easy.* Goyal Publishers, 2014.
2. **Green, Sharon Weiner.** *SAT Critical Reading Workbook.* Barron's Educational Series, 2013.
3. **Adler, Mortimer J., and Charles Van Doren.** *How to Read a Book: The Classic Guide to Intelligent Reading.* Touchstone, 1972.

Time Management Techniques

1. **Allen, David.** *Getting Things Done: The Art of Stress-Free Productivity.* Penguin Books, 2015.
2. **Clear, James.** *Atomic Habits: An Easy & Proven Way to Build Good Habits & Break Bad Ones.* Avery, 2018.
3. **Covey, Stephen R.** *The 7 Habits of Highly Effective People: Powerful Lessons in Personal Change.* Simon & Schuster, 1989.

Stress Management During Exams

1. **Davis, Martha, Elizabeth Robbins Eshelman, and Matthew McKay.** *The Relaxation and Stress Reduction Workbook.* 7th ed., New Harbinger Publications, 2019.
2. **Bailey, Chris.** *The Productivity Project: Accomplishing More by Managing Your Time, Attention, and Energy.* Crown Business, 2016.
3. **Weisinger, Hendrie, and J.P. Pawliw-Fry.** *Performing Under Pressure: The Science of Doing Your Best When It Matters Most.* Crown Business, 2015.

Websites

1. **Official ASVAB Website.** U.S. Department of Defense, www.officialasvab.com.

2. **ASVAB Career Exploration Program.** U.S. Department of Defense, www.asvabprogram.com.

3. **Headspace.** Mindfulness and Meditation App, www.headspace.com.

4. **Calm.** Mindfulness and Meditation App, www.calm.com.

5. **Insight Timer.** Meditation App, www.insighttimer.com.

ENHANCING YOUR ASVAB JOURNEY WITH EXCLUSIVE RESOURCES

I have curated additional resources for you as part of our commitment to your ongoing success and growth in preparing for the ASVAB exam. These resources are tailored to support your continuous improvement and help you navigate the complexities of the ASVAB with greater ease and confidence.

BONUS 1: 2500 Questions and Answers Explained

- **Master Key Concepts:** Utilize this extensive collection of 2500 questions and detailed explanations to reinforce and review essential topics covered in the "ASVAB Study Guide."
- **Effective Learning Tool:** Our comprehensive questions and answers are a proven method to enhance memory retention and recall, making your study sessions more productive.
- **Portable and Convenient:** Study on the go! Access these questions and answers from anywhere, allowing you to make the most of your time, wherever you are.

BONUS 2: Customized Student Planner

- **Stay Organized:** Keep track of your study schedule, exam dates, and important deadlines with our specially designed student planner.
- **Tailored for Success:** This planner includes sections for goal setting, progress tracking, and reflection to help you stay focused and motivated.
- **Visualize Your Progress:** With our planner, you'll be able to see your journey toward exam readiness, helping to boost your confidence and determination.

BONUS 3: Audiobook Version to Study On-the-Go

Complement your learning with an audiobook version, perfect for auditory learners and those with busy schedules who want to study while commuting or during downtime.

To access these exclusive materials, designed to complement your learning and development, **scan the QR code below.**

GET YOUR EXTRA CONTENTS NOW!

TO DOWNLOAD YOUR BONUS SCAN THE CODE BELOW

This bonus is 100% FREE, no strings attached

Or visit: https://rebrand.ly/615c65

We Value Your Feedback!

We're confident that our ASVAB Study Guide and bonus materials will help you succeed on your exam.

Your success is our priority, and we hope these resources are making your study journey easier and more effective.

If you've found our guide beneficial, we'd love to hear your thoughts! Leaving an honest review on Amazon not only helps us continue to improve our products but also guides other students in choosing the right resources.

Thank you for your support, and we wish you the best of luck with your studies!

TO LEAVE YOUR REVIEW

SCAN THE CODE >>>

Or visiti: **https://rebrand.ly/gqxaul3**

195

Made in the USA
Middletown, DE
10 December 2024

66565497R00108